TI
THRESHOLD
OF
PARADISE

David Jones

ORIGINAL WRITING

ISBN: 978-1-908477-29-3

A CIP catalogue for this book is available from the
National Library.

Published by ORIGINAL WRITING LTD., Dublin, 2011.

Printed by CLONDALKIN GROUP, Clonshaugh, Dublin 17

To

Fergus

Happy New
Year

From

Tommy C

FOREWORD

The verse contained in the present volume was composed between 1980 and 1984, often under difficult circumstances, as may be picked up from an attentive reading of what is written between the lines, the reason being that the very notion of literary activity was not particularly encouraged in the context of the Carthusian cloister, at least in the early eighties in France.

It is hardly an exaggeration to note that the problem of the compatibility or otherwise of literary output with the strictly contemplative life became in this instance a veritable "test case". This case was subsequently picked up and studied in detail by a very competent scholar, Eva Schmid (later Schmid-Mörwald), who produced a magisterial and balanced doctoral thesis on it at Salzburg University, published in 1994 under the title *The Lyre and the Cross: Incompatibility or symbiosis of the poetic vein and strict monasticism in the poetry of Alun Idris Jones, a Welsh Novice Monk*. It is hoped to reprint this study in the present series, with Original Writing, Dublin.

To resume the problem in a few words, it is as follows. The contemplative life in its purity seeks no justification for its existence outside the rights of the Creator, to whose gratuitous praise and adoration it has to be exclusively orientated. It is seen as an anticipation of the future life, and those who are called to that specific form of life within the Mystical Body are entrusted with a rôle on earth that corresponds closely to the rôle in heaven of the angels that are not called to intervene directly in the material service of mankind but only in the continuous praise of the thrice-holy God before His throne of Majesty. The creation and protection of an ambience in which this may happen is the very *raison d'être* of the claustral structure. Having been given the great boon of this structure in its purest form, that of the strictest Order in the Catholic Church, to seek then to pass once again from the entirely vertical to the partly horizontal, in the orientation of the powers and fruits of contemplation towards the literary service of Man, is to display an absence of purity of intention and even of faith and correct understanding of the rights of God over all for His own sake alone.

The concept is referred to as *Spiritual Virginity*, and it was studied and popularized by the deeply spiritual Jesuit author, R.P. André Ravier, confessor to the Grande Chartreuse. In a word, it can be summed up thus. The energy of the soul in the purely contemplative life belongs on every level to the One to whom it has been consecrated, and praise and adoration is purely gratuitous, because of the sovereign nature and therefore rights of the Creator. To "inquinate" or render impure, therefore, the limpidity of that mental and physical dedication and channelling of energy to anything but the Divine is to indicate that He is not sufficient for Himself, and that He has not the right to the exclusivity and totality of the powers and energies of a part of His creation, called apart for Him alone by choice of His Will and Providence.

That it is a valid line of thought is proven by the fact that much mental and even physical distraction and rechanneling of energy does in fact take place when meditation is no longer purely gratuitous, and when part of the mind's attention is drawn to think directly of Man and his needs.

However, the issue is not entirely simple, as another line of thought has been taken by St Thomas Aquinas, who in question 182 and following of the *Summa Thoeologiæ* (IIa IIæ), sets out to analyse the way in which it is actually superior not to be alight only but to be alight and also to shed light. It is the model contained in his famous expression, *contemplare, et contemplata tradere* (to contemplate, and to hand on the things contemplated).

Moreover, there was not unanimity within the Order itself on this line, as it was pointed out that historically it had not been without active engagement in the field of literary output, even from early times, and with considerable influence in that very field.

The particular situation of the author became uncomfortable, firstly on local level – he had been invited to burn or destroy poetic output – and then on the level of the Order's higher echelons (the Superior General had indicated that it might be sufficient to put away the already existing corpus without showing it again, but to obey with regard to future compositions). This explains why no more is written after 1982. The two which appear right at the end of the volume in 1984 were written precisely at the moment when he was told that the Superior General did not wish him to continue in the Order and renew his vows.

Curiously, both his own Prior and the Superior General were subsequently replaced with time, and their successors took a different line on the issues in question. In fact the local Superior invited Dom David to write to the General Chapter to ask for re-admittance to the Order, and it appears that the new Superior General, himself from Dom David's local Community, was open to the possibility, but the Definitory did not allow it, no doubt as a result of the message given previously by the former Superior General. This happened despite the request made at the same General Chapter by his former Master, himself by then Superior of another house.

All this took place several years after the initial drama, when Fr David was already a priest, but ill at ease because of the increasingly active orientation of the the Community to which he by then belonged, and where he was Novice Master. It explains how when, after the change of Superior at that house, and the subsequent change of functions within it, he asked if he could return to the eremitic life in Ireland, where he now is, in the grounds of a very ancient Celtic monastery, Duleek being by tradition the first stone-built church in the country, as the Gaelic name for the place suggests.

What had initially begun as a poem to accompany a melody composed by his mother, which despite its beauty did not succeed in gaining the prize at the National Eisteddfod, had become a factor at the level of interpretation of vocation. However, Providence was not absent from the meanderings of chance, and the harnessing of all the elements became possible through the openness of the kind Bishop of Meath, as also of close friends, such as John McKeever who suggested setting up the website which retains all the major sermons, and makes them available in audio or video form, or both, along with much other material of possible interest to visitors to the website, the address of which is www.frdavidjones.com.

Dom Augustin Devaux, his mentor in the Chartreuse, made a study of all the Latin poets of the Order in history (*La Poésie Latine chez les Chartreux, in Analecta Cartusiana*, 131, 1997), and concluded with a section on the latest period, finishing with Dom David. When sendng the book to him at his Ordination, he dedicated it in Latin with a quotation from a comment made by one who had read the volume: *Versiculi multissimi, poeta autem solus unus* ("so many verses, but only one poet" - the reference being to Dom David).

The verse composed and preserved in this volume saw the light of day thanks Dr James Hogg, who had himself been a junior professed monk of the same monastery, but earlier, and who became an important influence in the subsequent life of the author, both by his hospitality in the literary and academic field and by his human and even supernatural wisdom. The present volume was initially published under his editorship in the *Analecta Cartusiana* (129, 1988). It was the chance discovery of this volume that led to a student of his changing course in the choice of author for study. Being a student of profound interior life, she was well suited to the analysis of the subject matter. Her only regret was her inability to enter into the specifically Welsh domain, although she did spend time researching Welsh culture in depth in key centres of that culture in the summer of 1990.

She summed up her studies in one verse chosen from the sonnets composed by then:

... For depths with ink embrace.

THE
THRESHOLD
OF
PARADISE

Ausculta. Ausculta, fili mi,
Verborum conchas aperi,
Ne in his se abscondat Veritas
Et Transeuntem transeas.

Va lentement, va lentement,
Respire, aspire doucement
La grâce d'une vérité
Échappée de l'éternité.

Whoe'er thou be that readest this,
Tread slowly, softly – for the kiss,
The sense, the inward sense, the bliss
Of passing Truth much haste did miss.

Clyw, aros, clyw, ac aros eto awr
Gyfoethog yn ei hedd, a'r bedd a ddaw
Heb ruthr am a ddaeth, cans yma iaith
Adweinir lle cyffyrddwyd rhyw hoff baith.

ALL SAINTS' DAY
(1980)

Lord, through this cloister walked that sacred band,
Slowly they journeyed to another land.
Ties, honours, joys, past sweetness, far behind,
Onwards they marched, a better Home to find.

Each pointed hood concealed a world of thought,
Each hidden breast its war with Darkness fought.
Who shall e'er know the pains, the joys each knew?
Brother with brother could here share so few.

For as they walked, eyes lowered to the ground,
Sealed were their lips to every earthly sound:
To Thee alone dimmed eyes they fain would raise,
Their voice was consecrated to thy praise.

Onward and onward they on these stones moved,
Here where I tread, in ways past days have grooved –
Days that have dawned and ne'er shall dawn again,
For Night hath soothed awhile this hidden pain.

(Melody: *Navarre*, 213,
Welsh Baptist Hymnal)

LE JOUR DES MORTS

Gorchuddia'r pridd weddillion llawer sant;
Ni chlywir mwy eu lleisiau yn ein siant.
Ddoe canent yma wrth ein hochr ni –
Heddiw mae'u moliant ger y orsedd di.

Ddydd ar ôl dydd rhodiasant ger dy fron;
Olion eu traed sydd ar y garreg hon.
Pob peth cyfarwydd gynnau iddyn nhw
A ddaeth yn rhan i ninnau drwy'r tri llw.

Hwy ffoisant rhag holl degwch daear lawr;
Eu penyd hwy a drodd yn elw'n awr:
Yr hyn a welent gynnau drwy ddrych ffydd
Drwy dragwyddoldeb eu diddanwch fydd.

Mawredd y rhain i'r byd anhysbys oedd,
Llwyfan neu 'sgrîn ni wybu'u huchel floedd.
Nid oes na Dydd nac Enw ar eu croes:
Cadwyd eu coron hwy at arall oes.

Gwae ef, y neb a swynwyd gan dy Wedd,
Canys ni wybydd eto unrhyw hedd
Hyd oni thorro'r ffiol wrth dy draed...
– "O'r cyfryw drysor y fath golled waned!"

(Tôn: *Navarre*, rhif 213, *Llawlyfr Moliant*)

NOSON O DACHWEDD

Wrth im edrych tua'r nefoedd
Ar fin nos,
Seren dlos,
Teithiaf i'th bellteroedd.

Ti yn unig welir heno:
Gwena'n fwyn
Er fy mwyn –
Nid oes arall yno.

Pa le buost, ffyddlon gannwyll,
Ers y ddoe,
Ers it ffoi
I'th guddfannau tywyll?

Neu ai ti a welais hefyd
Cyn y wawr
Fel yn awr
Ar dy daith i'r Gwynfyd?

Fespera, fy annwyl gyfaill,
Gwn dy fod
Uwch y rhod
Wrth fy Nuw yn sefyll.

7/11/81
(Tôn: *Thanet*, 414)

Petit Été de S. Martin

Let me gaze into th'Empyreon
T'ward the Night,
T'ward this Light,
Child of old Hyperion.

Little, little spark of being,
Burn away
Night and day,
For thy Maker tarrying.

Is it far to where thou burnest?
Where in time
Should I climb
To be where thou sojournest?

For 'tis history that meets me
In thy rays:
Ancient days
Travel through Eternity.

All alone in heaven's stillness,
Quiet light,
Neon might,
Twinkle through Time's emptiness.

Self-consuming helion fission,
Dynamite,
Crack the Night,
Shout in starlit unison.

First and last of luminaries,
Call thy friends
From the ends
Of Time's unset boundaries.

Alpha, thou art Matutina,
Calling Dawn,
Hailing Morn,
Flooding Sleep's sealed retina.

And at dusk thou leanest o'er us
As the Earth
Tastes Night's mirth:
Omega, thou'rt Hesperus.

Faithful harbinger of glory,
Evening Star,
From afar
Call, call out from history.

Call us homeward to the Silence:
Bid us pause
'Neath the Cause
Of Time's short-lived turbulence.

(Melody: *Thanet*, 414)

AR ÔL CLYWED AM FARWOLAETH
Ewythr Mansel

Wrth godi heno'i olwg syn
At ddyfnder y dyfnderoedd hyn,
'Mhell, bellach fyth i'r pellter maith
Â'm hysbryd ar ei estron daith.

Pa beth, Dduw Gwyn, pa beth sydd draw,
Pa beth sydd uchod, fry, uwchlaw
Yr hyn a wêl fy llygad gwan
Wrth chwilio'r waharddedig Lan?

Chwi dawel sêr! Oes i chwi sain?
Wrth droi, wrth losgi yn eich blaen,
A wyddoch bellter ffin y rhod?
A deithiwch hyd derfynau Bod?

A fedrwch ddweud pa ryfedd dir,
Pa gaeau o oleuni pur
Oleuir lle na chyrraedd sêr,
Ymylir gan Gyffyrddiad Nêr?...

A all fod acw heno'n awr
Ryw newydd seren, newydd wawr,
Rhyw wên a wenodd arnaf fi
Yn gweld y Wên a'n creodd ni?

14/11/81

7

LAVELINE DEVANT BRUYÈRE
(Vosges)

As-tu chanté, jeune prêtre,
À Laveline,
Seul, ici devant ton Maître,
À Laveline,
Ces douceurs eucharistiques,
Ces récits évangéliques
Qui se montrent authentiques
À Laveline?

Cette négligence heureuse
À Laveline,
Cette invention désastreuse
À Laveline,
Prévue par la Providence,
Guidée par sa Main d'avance,
Prêche au monde sa Pésence
À Laveline

Vieilles vitres, carbonisées
À Laveline,
Chaire sculptée, pulvérisée
À Laveline,
Cloches fondues, tombées, cassées,
Poutres, orgues, croix entassées, –
Tout crie: *Assez! Assez! Assez!*
À Laveline.

Assez pour l'annihilation
À Laveline,
Assez pour une indication
À Laveline
Du degré de la fournaise
Qui ne laissa que des braises
Pour que l'érudit se taise
À Laveline.

Dans un tabernacle carré
À Laveline
Quelques petits cercles croisés
À Laveline
Crient, sans bruit, sans violence,
Dans un Éternel Silence:
N'aie pas peur, beau feu, avance!
À Laveline.

Petit tabernacle boisé
À Laveline,
Petits, petits cercles croisés
À Laveline,
Resté jaune comme l'arbre,
Restés blanchis comme marbre,
Restez-là. Que se délabre
Tout Laveline.

(Après un spaciment, 1981)
(Mélodie: *Wynnstay*, 400)

Le Père Prieur, qui vient d'apprendre cette nouvelle, en a été prondément touché. Il disait souvent la messe dans cette église aussitôt après son ordination. Il pense que ce serait sans doute l'électricité installée par le vieux curé qui aurait été la cause du désastre. Bien que ceci eût lieu il y a déjà plus de trois ans (en 1978), ce n'est que maintenant qu'il l'apprend. Les dégats sont evalués à un million. Le toit est tombé, et tout – complètement tout – est entièrement consommé par le feu, sauf le Saint-Sacrement et le Sacré-Cœur, qui restaient miraculeusement intacts, de même que le tabernacle en bois qui contenait le premier. Les Hosties ne portaient même pas de trace de brûlure.

MACHLUD HAUL

Daeth pen y dasg, daeth tirion olau'r hwyr –
Daeth terfyn dydd.
A ddaw yn ôl? – Na, fe ddiflanna'n llwyr,
Fel pob peth sydd.
Awr fesul awr, aeth bore yn brynhawn:
Gorffennol fu;
I ba ddyfodol awn?

'Rôl machlud haul, dros ffridd a ffordd a fflur –
'Rôl terfyn dydd,
Daw oriau'r nos, â'u mwynder hwy – a'u cur
I'r galon brudd.
Eu distaw su sy'n sibrwd yn fy nghlust
Am Un a fydd
I'r unig, 'r unig dyst.

Daw eto wawl, daw atom lewych gwawr –
Daw newydd ddydd.
Ar godiad haul mi deimlaf wefr yr awr –
Pa beth a fydd?
Awr dry yn ddydd, yn flwyddyn – ie'n fedd:
Un eiliad fer
A ddadorchuddia'i Wedd.

15/11/80
(noswyl penblwydd)

(Tôn: *Sandon*, 209)

II

EVE OF 27TH BIRTHDAY

Lord, o'er the hills the sun is setting fast –
         The day is done.
As twilight fades, it melts into the past,
         For ever gone.
Time with his quill hath noted every act,
         On this new page
       Recorded every fact.

Those silent cliffs shout back the Vesper peal
         Across the night,
And once again these hooded forms will kneel
         In failing light.
Lord, with the quire my voice to Thee I'll raise
         In ancient chant
       Of days of bygone praise.

For in this place, e'en for the book of Time,
         The story's told:
Known was this scent, this flick'ring light, this chime
         To those of old.
This eventide I do as they had done
         In eves long past
       Who morn high born have won.

                  (Melody: *Sandon*, 209)

TORIAD GWAWR

Daeth eto beraidd awr –
Do, daeth pelydryn gwawr,
Ac ynddo newydd obaith i drueniaid.
Drwy ddudew oriau'r nos
Marw fu bryn a rhos:
Daw hwn ag atgyfodiad i greaduriaid.

Pa beth a ddwg i mi?
Pa beth a'n herys ni? –
Dyfodol Dyn sy'n gwawrio dros y Cread.
I'r llanc, blas gwynfyd pur?
I'r llesg, dirdynnol gur? –
Ffyddlonaf dyst wyt, Haul, i bob dyhead.

Er pellter, lliw ac iaith,
Er brithder oed a gwaith,
Byw oriau'r Heddiw hwn wna pob creadur.
Dafn o'r diderfyn fôr,
Dawn yr anfeidrol Iôr,
Yw'r diwrnod hwn yn einioes fer pechadur.

Henffych it, Olau mwyn!
Henffych i'r hudol swyn
Sy'n cerdded heddiw'r bore drwy ein gofod.
Tyrd, Wawl, i'm calon i
Hyd awr dy fachlud di
Dros orwel pennod arall fydd yn darfod.

(Tôn: *Down Ampney*)

13

DAWN

(as church bell chimes 8 a.m., birthday)

Lord, in this gentle chime
I hear the heartbeat of Time,
And ponder: "Will that Hand e'er cease from giving?"
Now as I raise mine eyes
I see the sun arise
And in its rays new birth to all things living.

For 'tis thy mighty Hand,
As Dawn awakens our land,
That spins this tiny globe in due rotation.
Lord, as those stars depart,
Light floodeth this grey heart
The Light that bringeth life to all creation.

For every flow'r that grows
And every river that flows
Draws all its strength and pow'r from this Star's turning;
And whence could come its rays,
If, on that first of days,
Thy gleam had not enkindled its fair burning?

Hail to thee, new-born day! –
O powers of darkness, give way!
Sweet Light! Shine in the heart of all my brethren,
And find us at thy close
Peaceful in our repose,
Our souls bathed in the light of new-born children.

(1980)

(Melody: *Down Ampney*)

CASTELNAU DE GUERS

Vis-tu encor sur nos autels,
Doux Créateur de l'univers?
Se peut-il qu'ici l'Éternel
De nouveau se soit découvert?

Ô Castelnau! Si j'avais su
Qu'à cette heure, en ce lieu obscur,
Le Caché allait etre vu,
J'eusse escaladé ces gros murs.

Trop tard! Le Roi passe une fois,
Imprévu, sans le moindre éclat,
Pour rallumer ma tiède foi...
Il était là! Il était là!

... Ou devrais-je imiter ce saint
Qui – sachant ce qui était là –
Ferma les yeux et se retint:
«Mieux vaut la nue foi ici-bas».

Ce saint: Monsieur Jean Hubert, au miracle des Ulmes: apparition
semblable à celle-ci, laquelle fut vue pendant une heure par toute
la paroisse. Cf. aussi le saint roi Louis.)

GWYL CRIST FRENIN

Ai hwn yw'r diwedd, Frenin Nef,
A glywir sain y daran lef?
A dorrodd gwaedlyd wawr dydd Brad?
Ai dyma ddechrau'r erchyll Gad?

"Gwaed megis afon," meddai'r llais,
"Artaith yn feistr, trefn yn drais,
Storom ar storm o ddistryw'r Fall,
Ymdaith y grymusterau dall.

"Ddynion, a wyddoch beth sydd draw?
Oni ddyfalwch beth a ddaw?
'Heddwch', 'Tangnefedd', glywir byth.
Ffyliaid, na welwch heibio'r rhith!

"At ba beth y cronnir egni cudd,
At beth y dofir ynni'r pridd,
I ba les plethu'r ddichell hon,
Onid er ffrwydro'r blaned gron?

"Gwelwch yn fuan uwch eich pen
Arwydd o dân yn ysu'r nen:
Ddeng awr a thrugain pery'r wyrth,
Yna bydd Angau'n gwarchae'ch pyrth.

"Na! Na! Mae mwy! Mae gwaeth i ddod:
Ar ôl yr Arwydd yn y rhod
Natur ei hun a gyll ei phwyll,
  Suddo wna'ch pelen fach i'r gwyll.

  "Crefftweithiau coethaf Dyn â 'ngholl,
Daeargrynfâu a'u llynca oll.
Codi wna'r môr o'i drymgwsg maith,
Teithio wna'i ddwfr ar estron daith.

  "Gwaeth! Eto gwaeth! Gwaeth fyth a ddaw:
Dilyw o ddistryw sydd gerllaw.
Seinia'r apocalyptaidd awr,
Datrwymir clo'r Datguddiad Mawr.

  "Cans hon yw'r weledigaeth gudd
Welwyd gan ffyddlon dyst y Ffydd
Ar ynys fach mewn oes a fu
Rhwng pedwar mur unigedd du...

  "Awn yn fy mlaen, ond i ba les?
Oes un a gredo'r hyn ddaw'n nes
A'n nes, nes fyth bob awr sy'n dod,
Sef dechrau diwedd oll sy'n bod?"

Aros, atolwg, dyner chwaer!
Cyn mynd, dwed a ddaeth i ti air
Am awr neu ddydd, am amser, lle?
Pa beth sibrydodd Mam y Ne'?

"Un peth yn unig ddaeth i'm clyw,
Un peth ddatgelodd Mam fy Nuw
Rhwng dagrau twym ei chalon bur
Cyn dychwel i'w chuddiedig gur:

'Na chwilied neb nac awr na dydd:
Un neges rôf: mai hyn a fydd.
Tybiwch bob bore'n olaf wawr:
Ond felly'ch cedwir pan ddaw'r awr.' "

(Tôn: *Hesperus*)

CHRISTUS REX

Is this the end, O King of Kings?
This word that in my hearing rings –
"Filled is the cup; the time has come" –
Is it Thy last o'er crumbling Rome?

O Helena, unlettered dame,
Did Jesus call thee by thy name?
Can it be that those ears have heard
Th'echo of Judgment's final word?

What doth await this sinking world?
Into what era are we hurled?
Doth here begin our hell on earth?
Is this incarnate Satan's birth?

What didst thou hear, O messenger?
What is the sign, the harbinger
Of the beginning of the end?
What warning will the heavens send?

"Burning on high ye soon shall see:
For seventy hours the light will flee.
All men on earth will see the sign –
Yet will one seek his Lord benign?

"Nay, 'tis too late. The measure's full.
E'en 'mid th'elect the lamp is dull.
Darkness hath reigned. The saints have failed.
Christians their Master have renailed."

And after this what didst thou see?
What, faithful soul, was shown to thee?
 "Things that my spirit fears to tell:
 Lo! here begins Earth's living hell.

 "Men from the North will fill our land,
Walking with Satan, hand in hand,
Now is let loose a cosmic fight,
Might soon will scream 'neath its own might.

"O'er Peter's dome will sickles throne,
 Faith by the rack will be o'erthrown.
 In many lands Revolt shall reign,
 Atoms of fire fall as the rain...

"Blood like a stream from street to street,
Children like lambs that heav'nward bleat...
Five parts of human kind shall die,
Whole nations in oblivion lie.

"Nay, there is more! This very world
Out of its orbit will be whirled.
Tremors will swallow countries whole,
Oceans will travel, mountains roll...

"Famines, diseases all unknown,
Man's finest works 'neath engines mown...
Onward! O cataclysmic Force!
Chaos, walk on! Achieve thy course.

"All then shall say, 'It is the end!'
For that her ways Earth would not mend.
Now, even now, the fight is on
'Twixt Lucifer and Mary's Son.

"I could go on, but will aught hear?
Will even this make one soul fear?
Nay, 'e'en My Priests no more can care' –
And thou, thou too'rt caught in hell's snare."

– Wait! Wait, blest seer! But one more word.
What of the date have thine ears heard?
"One thing alone did I retain;
This did the Truth to whisper deign:

'Search not ye out the hour, the day.
'Tis near – and ever nearer – nay,
Live this one as though 'twere your last,
If, when it comes, ye would hold fast.' "

(Melody: *Hesperus*)

Immaculée Conception

When I was young how simple things did seem:
Earth then did bathe in Heav'ns high gentle gleam...
Lord, why, oh! why did I not then perceive
How rich that Blessing I'll ne'er more receive?

Had I but one small moment to relive,
How, oh! how would I not Thee glory give!
Lord, my dear Lord, how blind I was to Grace
In those dim distant days spent 'neath Thy Face!

How blest the Flame that sparks that surgent gleam
Deep in the night of Earth's ethereal dream!
One tiny grain of Love's strange quick'ning leav'n...
One heav'nly hour hath made one heir of Heav'n.

New is the newness of deep-welling life,
Clear, undefiled by daylight's common strife.
O! little head, when dost thou 'gin to feel,
And when of what thou hast thy first glimpse steal?

Life! O! new life, behold the rays of day!
Spin, tiny world, on thine uncharted way.
Hour after hour drink Time's unebbing gift...
Each rising day that lovely head shall lift.

Bathe in the stream of freely given light,
See at thy feet Youth's garden of delight;
Grow, grow to fulness; grow to full-grown bloom
Ere thicken those great clouds of gath'ring gloom...

What wilt thou feel, small, uncreated Queen,
Waking to find what unearned favours mean?
– Yet is this not Life's crown each laurelled night,
Nirvana's child, made for unmade delight?

...Were I a cell of embryonic Hope
That with its new-found gift of life did grope,
With my first breath this would be my first word:
"Fairer than all I thought is this fair world."

Nay, no more now may I one hour recall:
Each closing day's one more enclosing wall.
Once, only once, is each blest hour bestowed –
Grace! Grace! In vain thine unused flood hath flowed

Yet is it true that Youth is wholly o'er?
Calm unborn years, what holds your pregnant store?
Lord, is life lived, or is it just begun?
O Mystery of Life! Where wilt thou run?

(Melody: *Eventide*, 211)

Histoire vraie

Jeune honme, que tu dansais bien!
Ton jeune cœur battait si fort
Quand, serrant ce céleste lien,
L'Amour rapprochait vos deux corps!

Pays de rêve et de couleur,
Ton avenir s'annonçait beau:
Tu sentais déjà sa douceur
En palpant cette tendre peau.

La douce extase de l'amour
T'emportait vers dex cieux nouveaux:
«Le Paradis! – Et pour toujours!
Ce sera beau! Si beau! Si beau...»

... Ô Poudrier, tu savais peu
La force de ta suavité:
Ce parfum qui s'emparait d'eux
Décidait leur éternité.

Plaisanterie qui coûta cher!
Ces quelques grains de vanité
Que son haleine envoie en l'air
Retombent lourds de vérité.

«Poussière, ô homme, souviens-toi,
Tu étais et tu redeviens!» –
Écho lointain de cette Foi
Qui sait résonner chez les siens.

Ô Poudrier! Ô Poudrier!
La Grâce est sortie de tes grains:
Un demi-tour... Ces souliers
Qui dansaient iront danser loin...

La Trappe! accueille qui te vient
Envoyé par un poudrier...

Jeune homme? – Non! Il redevient
Ce qu'il eût voulu oublier.

DYDD NADOLIG

O Geidwad mwyn, Achubydd drud,
A glywi heno riddfan byd
Sy'r awr hon, tra'r addolwn ni,
Yn ochain am d'ymweliad di?

– Y llanc yng nghrafanc pleser sur,
– Y llef heb glust a glywo gur,
– Y llesg yn ei ddiderfyn boen,
– Y llon yn ei ddigysur hoen...

Pa win, pa wledd, pa wynfyd sydd
Heb flas o uffern ynddo 'nghudd?
Oes môr, oes man, oes modd, oes medd
I foddi'r llefain hwn am hedd?

Na, lleddf yw cân naturiol Dyn,
Ei ddyfnaf wefr dyf iddo'n flin:
Mewn gobaith am yfory gwell
Afrada'i oes mewn breuddwyd bell.

Ni wêl, ni wêl mai hon y'r awr
Yr ymgusana nef a llawr,
Y torrir argae'r galon drist
Dan fôr diatal gras ein Crist.

Ie, tyred, tyred, Feddyg byd,
Dos, rhodia heno sgwâr a stryd
Dinasoedd digonolrwydd Dyn
A gollodd oll o'i golli'i hun.

1980
(Tôn y Tad Laurence)

CHRISTMAS NIGHT

O Lord, sweet Lord, most precious Lord,
This night the world hangs on Thy word:
In moonlit vigil hill and dell
Await with me the matin bell.

Creation now in travail groans,
Earth's weary soul in sorrow moans;
Man's throbbing heart, with each new thrill
Unsated, pants and hungers still.

Mankind's eternal song is sad:
The dying man, the growing lad
– Nay, e'en the infant in the womb –
Each hour draws closer to the tomb.

The time is short, the time is short:
It is a whim, a passing thought
Dreamt by a moment that paused not,
But passed, and e'en its thought forgot.

And e'en the thought of ecstasies
Known once and left beyond the seas
That separate our yesterdays
Stands dim 'neath long a morrow's gaze.

The darkness of Man's darkest night
Awaits the uncreated Light:
Arise, great Orient – all is still –
Earth's silent dreams this night fulfil!

(Father Laurence Bévenot, OSB., has since set this to music.)

NOS GALAN

Ond eiliad fer, un eiliad fer
  Yn llithro drwy'r distawrwydd:
Y cyfan sydd, y cyfan fydd
  Sydd yn ei thic cyfarwydd.

   Awr! Awr! Clyw daro'r awr –
  Dyfodol holl drigolion llawr:
    'Nawr, 'nawr, i fawr a mân,
  Daw dalen lân o hanes.

O aros ennyd, eiliad chwim,
  Rho gyfle im dy ganfod.
Dy fesur di ni fedraf i,
  Na chydio yn dy hanfod.

   Awr, awr... – Pa beth yw awr?
 – Presennol oesoedd nef a llawr:
    'Nawr, 'nawr i fân a mawr
  Fe ddaw'r un treiglad Amser.

Un eiliad fer wna flwyddyn gron –
  Yfory ddaw yn Heddiw:
O ddydd i ddydd i'r oesoedd fydd
  Dilynnwn rawd y rhelyw.

Awr, awr... – Clywch droedio'r awr
Sy'n cyrraedd cyrrau pella'r llawr:
' Nawr, 'nawr, i fân a mawr,
Daw gwawr rhyw gyfnod newydd.

Bu amser – do, bu oesoedd maith –
Y bûm i ti'n absennol:
Fe ddaethost ti, fe aethost ti;
Ymdoddaist i'r gorffennol.

Awr, awr, ddiddychwel awr,
Dos, cerdda ar hyd wyneb llawr:
'Nawr, 'nawr, i fân a mawr,
Daw awr nas gwelir eilwaith.

Ble'r oeddit ti cyn cynnau'r sêr? –
A fu it enedigaeth?
Pan beidi di, beth ddaw i ni,
Pa ryfedd weledigaeth?

Awr, awr, ddiamser awr,
Cyfrifydd oesoedd daear lawr:
'Nawr, 'nawr, i fawr a mân,
Daw cân hen Dragwyddoldeb.

Ie, tyred ataf, orig fwyn,
　　Dy wefr rho im synhwyro;
Dy drydan di a'm treiddia i –
　　Â Amser drwy fy nwylo.

　　'Nawr, 'nawr, mae eto awr
Ail gyfle tra bwy'n rhodio'r llawr.
　　Awr... awr... ac eto awr –
A gwawria Tragwyddoldeb.

　　1980-1981
　　(Tôn: *Greensleeves*, 477)

New Year's Eve
(1980)

What sound, what distant melody
Steals thus upon my hearing?
– The hourly chime, the voice of Time
Its ancient message bearing:

> Now, now, this very Now –
> The sole through all eternity –
> Once, once, will it come to me;
> This Now must I live, not the morrow.

As hour by hour the past is spun,
Our future Time is weaving:
Each pain, each fight, each sweet delight,
Once gone, flees all retrieving.

> Now, now, this very Now –
> The sole through all eternity –
> Once, once, will it come to me;
> This Now must I live, not the morrow.

From day to day, in endless coils,
This globe is ever turning:
'Twill flee the night and seek the light
Till Dawn yields up her burning.

Now, now, this very Now –
The sole through all eternity –
Once, once, will it come to me,
This Now must I live, not the morrow.

Here with the year my life slips by
Each flow'r must slowly wither:
From op'ning womb to gaping tomb
O! Time, lead on, lead thither...

Now, now, this very Now –
The sole through all eternity –
Once, once, will it come to me,
This Now must I live, not the morrow.

(Melody: *Greensleeves*, 477)

Nos Galan, '81/'82

(wrth iddi daro deuddeg)

Ddigyfnewid weddi'r oesoedd,
Cwyd dy gân
Henaidd, lân
O'r di-ddydd amseroedd.

Heno clywaf a'r a glywodd
Yn dy sain
Rai o'r blaen
A fu'n teithio trwodd.

Canys ymdaith ydyw amser:
Yma'r af,
Yma caf
Ennyd eiliad Pleser.

Ie, unwaith deuaf yma –
Fel hwynt-hwy:
Aent oll drwy
Lidiart ein diddymdra...

Ddigyfnewid weddi'r oesoedd,
Cwyd dy gân
Fel o'r bla'n
I'r targwyddol lysoedd.

(Tôn: *Thanet*, 414)

New Year's Day, '81/'82

As I survey what hath gone by,
Each full-burnt dawn that now doth lie
In embers, seems as 'twere to sigh:
    "I once had been."

Each rising hope sunk in despair,
Used – nay, abused, beyond repair –
Cries from beneath th'horizon there,
    "These things have been."

Ah! Could I but begin again
Each ill-writ phrase that doth thus stain
These leaves of history that wane
    'Mid what hath been!

Nay, nay, alas! This ink clings fast:
Indelible, this script will last
From age to age, to th'ageless past
    Of what hath been.

As I reread Time's history
In this strange, timeless monast'ry,
Each sheet enshrouds one mystery:
    "Could else have been?"

Now as I turn the hours, the days,
As on each distant page I gaze,
This welling sigh my thought betrays:
    "It could have been!"

This book knows of another – nay,
And that, another, lost for aye:
If follows *if*, as if to say,
    "If *if* had been..."

Each loaded possibility
Hovering in eternity,
Born of unborn Reality –
    Could it have been?

Chain linked to chain of unlived facts,
Destined, predestined free-will acts
That were not made, that Fate subtracts
    From what hath been...

Could these have been?... Thou see'st them all,
O Sovereign Mind – and yet, dost call
Out of all Time that one thin, small
    Thread that hath been.

"Thus shall Time be!" – This was the word
Unthought, unpainted darkness heard.
Cause of each cause, Thou art the Lord:
    Thy *Yea* hath been.

Ancient of Days, didst Thou e'er see –
Nay more, e'en ere Thou wast, decree
That one, sole, *possibility*
    That could e'er be?

(On original melody)

Eve of St Agnes

Is this the eve on which 'tis said
That sighing maids too long unwed
May dream, and, dreaming, find a hand
To lead them to the promised land?

O snoring World! In this deep night
Are many in this sorry plight?
Are many, many souls alone?
Are many couples only one?

And is there one that thought of me?
Should two that sleep this night be three:
The third the fruit of th'other two –
Two dreams in this strange eve come true?

AR ÔL DERBYN LLYTHYR MAM

Beth yw'r su sy' treiddio muriau
   Dudew, distaw'r llwydgell hon?
Pa fwyn lesmair drodd ddoluriu
   Calon meudwy's seindorf lon?
Beth yw'r main blygeiniol sisial
   Dorrodd ar f'unigaidd nos?
Pa bur ffrwd o ddyfroedd crisial
   Ganodd gan mor denau dlos?

Clywais adlais rhyw beroriaeh
   Annaearol uchod, draw...
Ar gyfeiliant digerddoriaeth,
   Ar amseriad oes a ddaw:
Clywais guro mân adenydd,
   Trawiad rhyw angylaidd draed,
Dawns ar ddawns ar uchel fynydd,
   Esgyn, disgyn, naid ar naid –

Llawenhaodd pellaf lysoedd
   Nef y nef; a chlywais gôr
Mynaich, engyl ein hynysoedd
   Acw'n llefain dros y môr
Arnaf fi, eu holaf alltud,
   Baban lleia'r Teulu maith;
Yn eu plith, llais Dewi... Illtud...
   Clywais acen f'annwyl Iaith.

Sôn a wnaethant am ddychweliad,
   Ail-ddisgleiraid Haul a fu;
Canent ddyfod dydd Ymweliad,
   Dydd rhyw Gennad oddi fry:
Safiad traed yr Un a garent
   Ar y pridd a gofiant oll,
Llewych lamp a hir alarent,
   Atsain Siant a aeth yngholl...

Ai breudwydio'r ydwyf heno,
   A'm hir hiraeth na mi'n drech –
Bellach nid oes arall yno,
   Na'r un su ond bythol sgrech
Gwacter gwag meudwyol furiau
   Dudew, distaw'r llwydgell hon;
... Nid oes cwmni ond doluriau
   Calon dyn, heb seindorf lon.

1982

(Tôn: *Blaenwern*, 328)

Ymweliad: 'Roedd sôn yn y llythyr am bosibilrwydd ymweliad Pabaidd. Cyfeiriad sydd yma at weledigaeth San Dominic Savio.

*(relating the Holy Father's Welsh lessons
with Andrew O'Neill)*

Can it be that distant shadows
   Lengthening 'neath this fair moon
Reach out o'er those far off meadows
   That once knew a fuller noon?
Is this night like any other
   In that land so near, so far?
Wales! O! Wales, my gentle mother,
   What did thy first beaming mar?

And that sacred, desecrated
   Soil that holy feet have trod,
That unsated, permeated,
   Thirsting, brimming land of God,
Can it hear the faint, faint anthem
   Growing stronger from afar:
Light on light, and there before them
   One phosphoric boreal star?

Sleeping graves, with weary members
　　Resting from the well-fought fight!
Stone on fallen stone remembers –
　　Dream, dream on with me this night:
Feel, feel well the aching imprint
　　Of the absence of those men;
Bid each name, each stone, each footprint
　　Preach in silence now as then.

For a hermit hears at moments
　　Sounds that haunt much barren ground.
Echoes linger where high torrents
　　Of fair praise our walls did pound.
Grace in ancient tones did travel
　　There where Beauty had a song:
Come, good Priest, tread, kiss this gravel
　　That for this hour waited long.

(Melody: *Blaenwern*, 328)

Histoire vraie, hélas

Mais où vas-tu, Napoléon,
Dans ce désert de froid cuisant,
Ravageant comme Apolyon,
Nous sauvant en tout détruisant?

Sais-tu ce qui t'attend là-haut
À Moscou – oui, et au delà –
Le Bien que t'envoient ces maux,
Le Destin qui t'accueillera?

Je n'y crois plus. Mon Dieu est mort.
Le Néant – voilà l'au-delà!
C'est moi le maître de mon sort.
Ma gloire est ici, ici-bas».

J'espère, ami, que c'est le cas:
Pour toi j'espère que ma foi
Se trompe – oui, que l'au-delà
Est vide – au moins, *au moins pour toi.*

Tu n'es pas seul, grand commandant,
Dans l'incroyance de ta foi,
Incroyant croyant au dedans
Ce qui est en dehors de toi –

Et pensant, par le simple fait
De ne pas croire, fuir la loi
Qui doit décider ton forfait,
La pliant à ta propre foi:

Tu n'es pas seul: car cette nuit
— L'ultime pour tes braves rangs —
Deux voix s'entendent, mais sans bruit,
Préméditant ce bain de sang:

Nous sommes sergents tous les deux,
Et au-dessus de tout cela:
La crainte qui s'empare d'eux
Est plutôt peur de l'au-delà.

L'effroi ne peut pas avoir part
À notre table en cette nuit:
On sait qu'à l'instant du départ
De l'esprit, le sommeil s'ensuit.

Sommeil profond — et pour toujours:
Voilà le tout. Quel "au-delà"!
Festoyons en ce dernier jour;
Engraissons ces bons vers là-bas!

– Et pourtant... Si l'on avait tort...
– Écoute, ami: si c'est le cas,
Et qu'il y a survie dans la mort,
On n'a qu'à frapper ce contrat:

Si l'un de nous part sous ce feu
Et laisse l'autre avec sa peau,
– Et s'il y trouve quelque dieu –
Qu'il vienne en dire à l'autre un mot.

– Entendu!»... Et ce fut la fin
De ce repas si sombre et gai
Qui pensait noyer sous son vin
Le tocsin de l'éternité.

Helas! Helas! Le sang coula.
Et sur deux blessés l'un mourut,
Et, sans grand choix, vers l'au-delà,
Sans savoir dormir, accourut...

Et laissa l'autre, un peu moins gai,
Et moins encore après le bruit
Qui cria de l'Éternité:

L'enfer existe...

                    Et moi j'y suis!

LAUDABILITER VIXIT

Dom Martin, comment savais-tu?
    Ces yeux fermés, qu'ont-ils pu voir
    En cet étrange, étrange soir?
        Dom Martin, qu'as-tu vu?

Dom Martin, comment savais-tu?
    Tu parlais peu – si peu, si peu…
    Chartreux muet, connu de Dieu,
        Dom Martin, l'inconnu.

Dom Martin, comment savais-tu?
    De dix-sept ans aux cheveux blancs
    Ni son ni bruit, hormis le chant
        Dom Martin, tu t'es tu.

Dom Martin, comment savais-tu?
    Un jour, sans moindre infirmité,
    Emporté par l'Éternité –
        «Dom Martin? Qui l'eût cru!»

Dom Martin, comment savais-tu?
    Descendu pour un bon repas,
    Tu pris ce pain dans l'au-delà,
        Dom Martin – et y bus.

Dom Martin, comment savais-tu?
    Ce calme prophétique écrit
    Laissé sans bruit, là, sur le lit,
        Dom Martin, je l'ai lu.

Dom Martin, comment savais-tu?
    Ce code qui est si obscur,
    Et pourtant, si serein et sur...
        Dom Martin! C'est si nu!

Dom Martin, comment savais-tu?
    Ces mots d'adieu écrits pour nous
    Révèlent tout... et cachent tout.
        Dom Martin, qu'as-tu su?

Dom Martin, comment savais-tu?
    Ce testament fait dans la nuit,
    Cet *au revoir au ciel* sans bruit,
        Dom Martin, m'a ému.

Dom Martin, comment savais-tu?
    Ce mot ultime si discret:
    Le silence est le grand secret –
        Saint Martin l'a vécu.

(Dom Martin Sourdat est le seul père mort depuis mon entrée. C'est un saint incanonisé – disait Dom A., quand il était encore en vie – mais muet, tout à fait muet». On a trouvé son corps à côté du guichet.)

On hearing of Roger Howells' tragic illness

Art thou a priest, O man of God,
That liest on this bed of pain
Awaiting th'eerie Reaper's nod
And medicating Fate in vain?

Thou leavest here no progeny,
For thou didst choose, as those above,
The blissful double agony
Of love denied for scalding Love.

Unwed – nay, better, *celibate*, –
Each day clad in the livery
Of churchmen that thy church did hate,
A priest in sooth and verily.

Thou knewest that the Truth did lie
Amid the shelves of history,
And yet couldst hear Tradition's cry:
"Dost work my Sacred Mystery?"

And when, signed with the crimson Rood And,
hid by cloud on thuric cloud
Of Awfulness, thy form hath stood,
Know'st thou to what thy head hath bowed?

... A saint we lose, well do I know,
And one that leaves with echoes strong:
"I go above to work below:
In Heav'n I'll still to earth belong."

But when thou'rt there, O man of God,
When eaten flesh tastes no more pain,
If thou canst gain thy Maker's nod,
Come, bring me word: didst bow in vain?

(C'est un jeune ministre de la haute église. Sa sainte préferée est
la petite Thérèse, laquelle disait aussi en mourant: «Je vais passer
mon ciel à faire du bien sur la terre».)

AR ÔL DERBYN ANRHEG ODDI WRTH FY MRAWD

Rhagluniaeth a 'sgrifennodd ers cyn cof
Y geiriau mân a ffurfiaf yma'n awr.
Myfi at wyryf ddalen lân a ddof
Er graddol osod cnwd fy mhen i lawr.
A roddwyf ar y ddalen hon ni wn –
Ni wyddwn 'chwaith cyn hyn rym Awen dlos,
– Ond darllen wnaethost Ti y cymal hwn
Pan oeddwn eto 'mherfedd perfedd Nos.
A thi, fy mrawd, wrth ddanfon ataf *ben*,
– O bosib' am na wyddet beth i'w roi –
A syniet mai cyplysu daer a nen
Â dolen-gyswllt drydan 'roeddet ddoe?
Cans ceg mudandod meudwy ydyw hwn,
A ddeil ar ei ysgwyddau 'nhrymaf pwn.

1982

AFTER RECEIVING HUW'S PRESENT
(By exceptional favour on the Prior's part:
«Mais dites-lui de ne pas en envoyer d'autres».)

A little gadget that can move the world,
An instrument of Man that men doth turn,
The voiceless herald of the silent word
That thou, whoe'er thou be, e'en now dost learn:
Its tiny body heaves my Now to thine
And freezes for e'ermore one drop of Time
As, senseless, marking line on senseless line
Of Meaning, it begets incarnate Rhyme...
And thou, dear brother, when thou thought'st of this
(Perchance not knowing what else thou couldst buy),
When thou didst choose these parting hearts that kiss,
Didst hear their little voices at thee sigh:
"We penetrate into a dumb man's cell,
Without a word his stifled words to tell."?

YR AIL O CHWEFROR

O olau mwyn, oleuni pur!
Gwasgara'r nos â'th lewych clir.
Abetha'n araf d'einioes gu,
Ymdodda yn d'oleuni di.

Ti fywiol fflam mewn tywyll dir,
Drwy'r caddug, ffyddlon dyst i'r Gwir,
O dysg im farw fel tydi –
Lleihau bob awr wna 'mhabwyr i.

Rhagflaenaist olau Blaen y Wawr;
Goleuni'r bobloedd ddaeth yn awr.
Diflanna, dirion ferthyr mud:
Dy gorff, fe'i llosgaist dros y byd.

O Grist, wir Haul, dyrchafwn di!
Tyrd, llenwa'n awr ein temel ni.
Disgleiria heddiw newydd Wawl;
Am weld dy Ddydd, dyrchafwn fawl.

A phan ddifodda'n cannwyll ni
Pan ballo'r llusern yn dy Dŷ,
Rhyddha dy weision di mewn hedd
I orffwys dan fwyn wawl dy Wedd.

(Tôn: *O lux beata*)

CANDLEMAS

O light, fair light, most gentle light!
Thy tiny flame o'ercomes the night.
Burn bravely on, 'tis nearly day;
The Light of lights is on His way.

How strange this dance, this restless play!
Each fight, each flicker seems to say:
"Behold how, slowly, I must die.
My life I burn, my end draws nigh."

How echoes thine unuttered word!
My usèd heart a toll hath heard.
Thy work is done, O candle bright,
Thy flame hath melted into light.

O noble sacrifice indeed!
O lesson for the world to heed!
Thou teachest me, O martyr sweet,
My life to lose in light and heat.

All hail, great Light, celestial Ray!
O Christ, Thou art the Break of Day!
At last these darkened eyes may see
The Dawn of Immortality.

Lord, when this flame is wholly spent,
And shadows bathe once more this tent,
In peace may we, at thy behest,
Go forth, and, 'neath thy radiance, rest.

Amen.

(Melody: *O lux beata*)

WAS IT THÉOPHILE GAUTIER?

Est-ce toi le poète qui sema ces vers
Qu'un beau jour, dans un livre que j'avais ouvert
Par hasard, je rencontrai et, les ayant lus,
Méditai longuement, dans un rêve éperdu?
Est-ce toi qui prononças ce verdict hautain
Sur ces rangs capuchonnés qui marchaient en vain
Vers le Néant qu'ils priaient – que tu connais mieux,
Éclairé que tu es par l'éclat lumineux
De la Raison.

O Philosophie Souveraine!
Connaissance assurée, connaissance certaine
Du plus grand Inconnu – connaissance, assurance
Dont la base solide est la ferme Ignorance,
Ta pitié pour ces gens que tu voyais assis
À leur *table frugale*, tous à la merci
D'une immense illusion, qui, hélas! aboutit
Au lugubre repas que ton barde décrit,
Me transperça le cœur, et me fit réfléchir
Sur mon âme et ma fin qui ne saura finir –
Et sur toi, ô grand juge, jugé maintenant,
Pèlerin éternel d'un lointain continent
Où se trouvent des gens qui ont marché en vain
Vers le Néant qu'ils priaient – ce Mythe enfantin
Qui t'exclut de leur nombre, et te laisse dehors,
Philosophe assuré, connaissant tout son tort...

... Oui, ta vie est vécue... Et la mienne conmence –
À la merci, hélas! d'une illusion immense
Ensemencée un jour par hasard par des vers
Que je lus dans un livre que j'avais ouvert.

AR ÔL DAMWAIN FEL *EXCITATEUR*

Wrth droi am byth y fythol droëll hon
Sydd, er nas gwyr hyhi, yn troi y Rhod,
Trof, trof yn ôl ar don ar gyson don
O ddigfnewid drai a llanw Bod
At ddechrau ail-ddechreuad dechrau'r dydd
Ddeffrôdd dragwyddol Nos o'i thrymgwsg du;
A theithiaf ar eu cefn i'r hyn a fydd –
Hiraethus gof pob atgof fyth a fu...
O! dyner Gloc, a wyddost mai tydi
Sy'n dal y llaw a'th ddeil, a'n troi a'th dry,
Mai'r tawel guriad dyr ar draws y si
Yn oriau'r nos, yw sain yr oriau fry
Lle nad oes dechrau ond dechreuad Nos
Na dderfydd byth, byth bythoedd, gan mor dlos?

1982

AFTER AN ACCIDENT AT *EXCITATIO*
(Community awoken two hours too soon)

I wind thee once again, sweet little clock,
And, winding, turn another full-writ page:
This grinding key one yawning day doth lock
To sleep 'neath the sarcophagus of Age.
Good night, good friend! I take a moment's rest,
Relying on thy faithful watch the while.
Tick on, tick on, tick on, tick on... on... – lest
I rave, unfrocked on Hypnos' desert isle...
– And fail to pull in time each little bell
That pulls a brother-lark from his soft planks.
Alarm me out of heaven into hell,
To shiver, yawn, and fragrantly give thanks
For what this world that those small fingers move
Forgets, while lying deep in unfelt Love.

Canol gaeaf

Distawrwydd perffaith heno sydd
Yn gwrando cân fy nghalon brudd:
Eisteddaf yn ei gwmni ef
Yng ngharchar carcharorion Nef.
Distawrwydd! O! ddistawrwydd pur,
A glywi di ei thawel gur?
A fyddi d ryw ddydd yn dyst
I aberth byw d'ysglyfaeth drist?

Ac eto, a yw hyn yn wir,
Mai creulon ydyw d'estron dir?
Ac oni chlywais yma gnt
Ryw siffrwd Traed, ryw nefol Wynt ?
Adenydd sy'n eich plith,
O Furiau! dafnau Gras yw'ch gwlith...
O Gell! O Gell! dy wacter du
Sy'n orlawn lys i glaerwyn lu.

Gwrandawaf heno ar dy sain,
Clustfeinio wnaf yn fanwl, fain:
Mae gennyt fwy i'm dysgu i
Na minnau ar dy gyfer di.
O! dysg, O! dysg im ymwacáu;
Ddiddymdra! Gwna im ymnacáu,
Diflannu, ymddistewi'n llwyr –
Ond llestr gwag crefft derbyn ŵyr.

Llonyddwch pur! – llonydda fi;
Rho glywed dan dy dyner si
Ryw neges o'r di-amser rod,
Ryw air o'r Gair a wnaeth im fod...
– " 'Rwy'n siarad," meddi wrthyf fi,
"Ond byddar wyt – rhy lawn, rhy lawn,
Rhy brysur fore hyd brynhawn."

Rhy hwyr! Rhy hwyr! Aeth Gras yngholl.
I ba le'r af â'm ffwdan oll?
Fy enaid, aros ennyd awr,
Yf hedd y nos cyn cyffo'r wawr...
O dawel sain! – tyrd, swyna fi,
Cans plentyn wyf i'th fynwes di:
Ohonot deuthm, ataf af –
Dawelwch! Caf, ryw ddydd fe'th gaf.

(Tôn y Tad Laurence: *Christmas Night*)

SEPTUAGESIMA

When sorrow paints its pale lament
In colours of the firmament,
When earth drinks deeply heav'n's dropped tears
And silence some great sighing hears,
And when, alone with Loneliness,
I think on what was happiness:
Then, then alone is all in tune,
Then doth my heart with Earth's commune.

For Sorrow is the world's refrain:
The melody of stifled pain
Recurring o'er the rhythmic years
On each new generation's ears
Re-echoes down Time's deep abyss
The hollowness of wanted bliss,
And cries to highest heav'n above
The void of love devoid of love.

O Fulness! Where is thy full source?
Encounter! Where thine untouched force?
The need of the unsatisfied,
Th'illusion of the falsified,
The Pleasure that no more doth please,
The thumping Pain that knows no ease
Screams, *No! No more... 'Twere better dead...*
O Sorrow! Thy last word is said.

Was it for this that Life was made?
Was earth for earth on this earth laid?
And did the Hand that took that clay
And bid it reckon Time's first day
Say, *Cursèd be e'ermore this seed:*
On Sorrow's bread alone 'twill feed
Till it return from whence 'tis come
– To emptiness, Fulfilment's home.?

(On original melody)

NOSON O AEAF

Mae hiraeth yn yr heddiw hwn
Am ddoe ac echdoe unwaith fu,
Ac er y llosgwyd hwy, mi wn
Nad diffodd ydyw atgof cu.

Hwy aethant, ddaethant, ddônt drachefn
Ar draws y gwacter leinw 'nghell:
Y pethau dybiwn fod o'm cefn
O'm blaen y meant, fel breuddwyd bell...
Ddydd ar ôl dydd ânt bellach fyth
I bellter y gorffennol maith...
'Mhell, bellach fyth... nes toddi 'mhlith
Y pellaf heddiw ataf ddaeth.

O Heddiw! Oni wyddost ti
Mai yn d'eiliadau prin, di-flys
Y nytha f'unig egwyl i
Rhwng ras a ras, rhwng brys a brys,
Mai'r ysdaid fer gymeraf 'nawr
Yn nyfnder nos, rhwng dydd a dydd
Yw dolen gyswllt gwawr a gwawr,
Man cychwyn Ddoe i'r Hanes fydd?

Pa beth fydd yn dy oriau di?
Pa Ddoe a grëi yn fy nghof?
Yfory eto wyt i mi:
At ddirgel ddalen lân mi ddof,
Heb wybod pa gymalau cudd
Ddarllenaf – na, 'sgrifennaf f'hun
Ar lyfr yr atgofion fydd
Yn fyw i'r 'Fory pellai un.

Edrychaf 'nôl, edrychaf 'mlaen...
Ail-fyw, rhag-fyw yw 'mywyd oll,
Ac yn fy rhag-gynllunio cain
Aeth Heddiw'r ddoe a'r echdoe 'ngholl.
Tydi, ti'n unig yw fy rhan –
Ni feddaf arall yn fy llaw:
Yr Yma hwn yw'r unig fan
Y dof o hyd i'r hyn a ddaw.

Boed imi flasu pob rhyw awr
A lithro drwy fy mysedd tlawd
Y diwrnod hwn – y mwyaf mawr
A fu, a fydd yn teithio'r Rhawd:
Cans teithio wna – a theithio'n glau –
'Run, unig Heddiw fyth caf fyw...
O! na ddysgaswn grefft mwynhau
Y fwyaf Rodd fyth roddodd Duw.

Daw dydd pan na ddaw mwy i'm rhan
Na ras na brys, nac ysbaid fwyn
Rhwng gwawr a gwawr, rhwng man a man,
Na dalen lân, ail-gyfle'n dwyn
I yfed gwefr yr orig hon
A logir im gan drefn y Rhod
'Nawr, yn fy nhro, wrth deithio'r don
Ylch oes 'rôl oes fenthycwyr Bod.

Mae hiraeth yn yr heddiw hwn
Am ddoe ac echdoe unwaith fu,
Ond, er ei ddeigryn ef, mi wn,
Bydd heddiw 'fory'n echdoe cu.

1982
(Ar dôn wreiddiol)

3 A.M.

O Silence deep... deep, deeper still...
O dew of Peace, thy peace distil;
Come, tingle softly in mine ears,
Thou Song of Time, voice of the years.
Thou art the hermit's company,
Of Solitude, the symphony –
O! soundless Sound, how strange thou art,
Thou searcher of the human heart!

O quietness! O quietness!
The language of Earth's loneliness,
Unchanging are the undertones
That echo 'twixt these changeless stones:
This night I hear what heard of yore
All they that came this way before –
Monk after monk sat where I sit,
As History by Time was writ.

I listen to the emptiness
That led these men to holiness;
I wait... I wait for some small word,
Some message from the great unheard –
And hear instead the noise within,
The rustling of the restless din
Of words... more words... more worrying,
And unbecalmèd hurrying.

O Buzz of solitary thought,
By thee my fathers here were taught:
The grammar of the art of pain
Doth sound, resound again, again –
Above, below, from wall to wall
Each inch of Cell doth seem to call:
Walk on, walk on where these have walked,
Like thee, they with these walls once talked...

Where are ye now, my brethren, where –
'Neath nameless cross so stark, so bare?
In death, e'en as in life forgot,
Your silent lives in silence rot...
– Our little brother, wait awhile:
These gaping skulls one day will smile,
Will hold thee close in tight embrace
In silent love's deep face-to-face.

(Melody: *Christmas Night*)

Diwrnod Ympryd ar Ganol Gaeaf

Llawenydd! Ti yw f'ymborth i
Ar lwyd ympryd-ddydd gaeaf llwm:
Mwyn flas d'amheuthun wacter di
Wna'n ysgafn bwysau'n penyd trwm.
Paham? Paham na theimlaf mwy
Yr ing ŵyr pob newyddian glas
Y dydd y treiddia gyntaf drwy
Y pyrth a geidw oes tu faes?

Ai am i'm gwawr weld tecach cell
Sy'n gweld a chlywed sêr y nen?
Ai am i'm Hedd gael muriau gwell
Sy'n adlewyrchu'r Drindod Wen
A'r Glendid deimlaf 'nawr o'm cylch
Dan ffrydlif dihidliadau'r Iôr:
Y gras ar ras a'm tawel ylch,
A'm trych yn nwfr heddychol fôr?

Neu a oes rheswm arall cudd
Am wawr rhyw newydd gyfnod mwyn
A machlud mebyd meudwy prudd –
Rhyw newydd ryddid, newydd ffrwyn
A'm tyn at ddydd na welwn gynt
Pan rois fy mraich i fraich y Groes,
A'm cipia'n chwa rhyw feddwol Wynt
O'r loes a ladd i'r Loes ddi-loes?

Newydd-der! Ail-ieuenctid! Gras!
Ni wn beth wyt, ond ildio wnaf
I'r rhyfedd fwyn benydiol Ias
Sy'n lladd er atgyfodi'r claf.
– Cans clwyfus fûm o'th glwyfau di,
A'm plygodd, torrodd gan mor drwm;
Ond heddiw blas dy gwmni dry
Yn wledd yr hyn oedd ympryd llwm.

1982
(Ar dôn wreiddiol)

Sunset on Septuagesima Sunday

We call thee Joy; but what art thou?
This blessedness that cometh now
And goeth then to whence it came,
What is it? What lies 'neath this name?
I know thee, and have known thee well –
And known a little of the hell
Where thou art not, where sweetness sours,
And Pleasure lives on borrowed hours.

Why may I never see thy face
Uncovered, nor retain th'embrace
Of waves of unexpected bliss
Aroused by thy soft fleeting kiss,
Giv'n always when I sought it least –
And never when I sat to feast
On what I thought was thy delight
In th'eye-to-eye of naked sight?

Elusive god, I worshipped thee –
As this whole world on bended knee
E'en now, from end to furthest end
Of heathen Christendom, doth send
One ceaseless mighty liturgy
In litany on litany
Of consummated sacrifice
To thine imagined Paradise.

I sought thee... and will seek again,
E'en though I know I seek in vain
Thy presence in th'e'er absent lust
Of dust for its own native dust –
Forgetting that thy blissful fire
Burns only when allumed Desire
Burns out, and, deadened, feeling nought,
Feels that for which it ever sought.

Noswyl San Ffolant

Yfory pa annisgwyl ras
A ddisgyn arnaf fi a thi?
Ai dydd fel arall yn y Clas,
A rewodd fyth ein dyddiau ni,
Ddaw fel y ddoe a'r echdoe cynt
Yn heddiw fel y llall i mi?
– A thithau ar wahanol hynt,
Pa wefrau rydd d'amrywiol sbri?

Amrywiaeth! Cofiaf gynt dy flas
Ar drothwy pob rhyw wawr fwyn gudd
A deithiai drwy'r uchelder glas
At ddunos calon fythol brudd,
Dan gludo yn ei mynwes lawn
Ryw stôr o ddigwyddiadau drud
Drysorwyd gan amryliw ddawn
Rhagluniaeth cyn bod gwawr ar fyd.

Amrywiaeth! Cofiaf weld dy wedd
Yn nhoriad gwawr Ieuenctid llon:
Y cyntaf brawf gaed ar dy wledd,
Y Darganfyddiad newydd sbon
O'r rhyfedd gyfoeth roddid im
Gan ryw gudd, faith haelionus Law
A'm tynnai o'm cysefin Ddim
Ar ryw bell, bell Nirfana draw.

Ie, darganfyddiad oedd y wawr
Ragflaenai ddydd ar newydd ddydd
O Hanes – un Gofynnod mawr
Uwch datblygiadau Tynged gudd...
Ond gydag arferolrwydd oes
Arferais ar arferiad hir
Y Rhodd ry rad yr hon a roes
Y Llaw a'm rhodd ar gyfryw dir.

Anghofiais bris y Fendith ddaeth
Yng ngwyn belydrau'r newydd wawr
A dorrai un, un unig waith
Ar lwybr un a rodiai'r llawr
Mewn rhyddid am ond cyfnod byr –
Cyn dilyn rhyw annisgwyl ras
At fan lle bellach byth ni thyr
Ond gwawr un bythol rewddydd Clas.

1982
(Ar dôn wreiddiol)

St Valentine's Day

When I remember this sweet day
That came, and came again each year
To winter, as some summer's day,
The heart of Youth once more to cheer,
That heart feels one small tiny twinge
Of Envy for what 'tis no more,
And all but rubs the naughty fringe
Of Longing for what went before.

For this wee tear that wells within
Springs from that same unchanged soft heart
That long ago, unversed in Sin,
Learnt early on that Bliss can smart,
And knew the meaning of Surprise
Unraved by such an ugly child:
Th'encounter 'twixt two loving eyes,
The sun that in a look once smiled.

And did the tree that gave its strength
To form that tiny cardboard square,
One inch in breadth, the same in length,
Placed shyly in that schooldesk there,
E'er dream what dreams its wood-pulp fed
In one so green, so unprepared
For news like this – that some heart bled
Of deepest love for love unshared?

O Shyness! How thy name is strange!
Blest Virtue, thou dost fire amiss!
... And didst Thou, Providence, arrange
Before all time that sudden kiss
Giv'n lips on lips, without a word
Of warning, to a little boy
That stood all stunned, all dazed, all blurred,
Too shy to answer, for too coy?

Or didst Thou, Providence, e'er Will
That that high grace should pass unclutched,
That those two hearts should part, until
For two whole years once more they touched,
Once more upon a schooldesk – but
Much older, fairer, riper – nay,
Too conscious of the wound once cut
To look, or smile, or bid *Good day*?

O Shyness! Thou hast done thy work!
Two ways have parted for e'ermore...
Yet this dumb tear that still doth lurk
Twangs loudly on the cords of yore.
O! human Heart, how strange thou art!
Or is it thou, strange Providence,
That dost estrange what must depart
For ever, *dans ce Grand Silence*?

WRTH GOFIO'R ALWAD DDENG MLYNEDD YN ÔL

Sŵn y gwynt a sisial Amser –
   Unig su'r gyfarwydd gell...
Lleisiau dyn, cyfaredd Pleser,
   Cilio maent ymhell, ymhell.
Heno, Arglwydd, unig ydwyf –
   Unig gyda'r Nef i gyd;
Tyrd yn agos, fel y teimlwyf
   Gwmni'r Un sydd fwy na'r byd.

Pam y dygaist fi i'r fangre
   Anghyfannedd, ryfedd hon?
Cysur ffrindiau, aelwyd, pentre,
   Holl linynnau'r galon lon...
Rhwygaist hwy, Berffeithiaf Feistr –
   Gwyddit nad ar ddafn mae byw,
Ond ar gariad pur, difesur
   Mynwes glyd yr unig Dduw.

Clywaf drydar ola'r adar –
   Mawl eu Crëwr yw eu cân;
Gyda hon fy hwyrol bader
   Gyfyd ar adenydd mân.
Entrych Nef mae'n tawel gyrraedd
   Megis aberth y prynhawn:
Thuser ydyw'n tarthu'n beraidd;
   Nef y nef sy'n agos iawn.

Agosâ, O ddwyfol Geidwad,
  Cwmwl Iâfe, tyrd i lawr:
Cuddiais gynt y ddau Geriwbiad;
  Llwyr orchuddia f'enaid 'nawr.
Gad im yfed eto'n helaeth
  Neithdar dy gyfriniol Waed;
Gad im wledda ar fy Ngobaith,
  Gorwedd, gorffwys wrth dy Draed.

Cau f'amrannau yn dy Freichiau,
  Teimlo gwres dy Law o'm cylch –
Hyn a ysgafnha fy meichiau,
  Hyn fy nyfnaf friw a ylch.
Nofio, boddi yn dy gariad,
  Heno wnaf ym môr d hedd,
Nes deffrowyf gyda thoriad
  Gwawr dy Wên a'th dyner Wedd.

(Tôn: *Diolch a chân*, o eiddo Mozart, 459)

NIGHTFALL, ST VALENTINE'S DAY
(Remembering the Call on this night ten years ago)

Silence... silence... deep, deep silence
  Seeps into my tingling ears;
All Earth's noise, all Pleasure's violence
  Shouts in vain across the years.
Here mine eyes meet thine, O Master,
  Here none other enters in ...
Broken lies the alabaster,
  Broken every tie with sin.

Evening gently bathes the cloister,
  Night envelops all Mankind.
Walls! Reclusion well you foster,
  Night! Beyond, what dost thou find?
– "Beds of pain, where Joy weeps, dying,
  Beds of bliss, unsated birth..."
Count the tears, record the sighing,
  Feel the pulse of youthful mirth.

Darkness stills the sounds of nature,
  Earth rolls on, asleep... asleep...
Lord, o'er each reposing creature
  We with Thee our vigil keep:
These deep tones resound in Heaven,
  Angels bear on high our prayer,
As the Breath to mortals given,
  Changed to Song, regains the air.

Shrouded now in black – nay, hidden
　　Are those works that fear the Light;
Lucifer's smooth hand has bidden
　　Draw the veils of thirsting sight.
Night, hide deep within thy bosom
　　Hours the sun would blush to see;
Youth, Love, Beauty, take seed, blossom
　　Trance ethereal, soon thou'lt flee.

(*Following morning at dawn*)

Night! O Night! Thy tight hold weakens
　　Truth is leaping o'er the hills.
Life, new life, Creation beckons,
　　Song, contagious, dances, trills.
Dawn, arise! These stone walls shatter!
　　Shine in this grey hermit's heart.
Heav'nly light, Hell's dank mists scatter.
　　Hail, fair Morn! Sweet Grace impart.

Unseen Light, thy pris'ner seeks Thee,
 All alone – alone with Time.
Siren Spell, Thy call hath chained me...
 Call! Call! Call! – like this strange chime:
Lord, it counts the hours that linger
 To the fall of endless Night:
Call me *then* – move but a finger
 Point me to the Walls of Light

(Mozart's tune, 459)

BENEDICITE

Fendigaid Un, bendithia † ni,
Bendithia'r fendith hon o li
Dwfn gefnfor maith bendithion pêr
Bendigedicaf Wynfyd Nêr.

GRÂCES

Diolchwn iti, radlon Dad,
Am rodd a roed in heddiw'n rhad,
Un awr – fel rhodd doe, echdoe gynt,
Â'u horig fwyn i'n horiog hynt.

(Tôn: *O lux beata*)

BENEDICITE

Bless † us, O highly blessèd One,
Bless what hath blest the gentle Sun
That rose again to bless the Earth
With rays of blessèd, blessèd Mirth.

GRÂCES

We thank Thee, Sun of Righteousness,
For moments of sweet Happiness
At morn, at noon, at eventide,
To mark Time's hourly ebbing tide.

(Melody: *O lux beata Trinitas*)

BENEDCITE

(dawn, mardi gras)

Bless † us, O highly blessed One,
Bless this new blessing of thy sun,
Ris'n once again to bless the Earth
With rays of richly blest new-birth.

GRÂCES

We thank Thee for this gift of love
Descending from those stars above
That now recede to where they were
Ere Love from Love for love did stir.

(Melody: *Iam lucis orto sidere*)

At Meditation

Colour of darkness, land of recollection,
Blindfold my senses, dampen each reaction,
Fasten the world: in one, one sole direction
    Draw all mine inwards.

O tranquil Void! Come, make my vision single,
Unruffled Calm, come, let me hear thee tingle,
Virginal Stillness, let me with thee mingle,
    Stepping in Silence.

Inward I walk, toward mine inmost kernel,
Deeper I dig, to summits, orbs supernal,
Each thick'ning hour I palp into th'Eternal,
    Walking on Absence.

Strange is the dark; and stranger is the darkness
That darkened minds unveil in their aloneness:
One with the One, all one with utter Oneness,
    Solitude thunders.

(Melody: *Christe Sanctorum decus Angelorum*)

MARDI GRAS

BENEDICITE
(noon)

Descend upon us, blessèd Grace;
Bless † with the blessing of thy Face
This restful boon that bids us pause
One hour, 'neath Time's unhurried Cause.

GRÂCES

We thank Thee, hidden Source of Good,
For this new gift of borrowed food,
Not ours to take, not ours to give –
No more than this new hour to live.

(Melody: *Rector potens*, ferial tone)

BENEDICITE
(evening)

O blessèd Light, whom now doth hide
The softer gleam of eventide,
Shed one more blessing † ere we go
To where Thou dreamtst us long ago.

GRÂCES

Arise, O Incense sweet, arise!
Rise, evening praise, embalm the skies!
The greatest gift at last is giv'n:
Riv'n grateful hearts for grace full riv'n.

(Melody: *O lux beata Trinitas*)

MERCREDI DES CENDRES

... And thank Thee for this hunger, Lord,
This void that savours thy sweet Word:
We feed on fasting for one day,
Lest we forget our tasteless clay.

(*O lux beata*)

DYDD MERCHER Y LLUDW

Anfeidrol Iôr, Greadwr Hollgyfoethog,
  A luniaist Ddyn o bridd a llwch y llawr,
Yng ngwawl dy Wedd, y Sanct, yr Hollalluog,
  Ond cysgod breuddwyd yw'r Bydysawd mawr.
     Gerbron dy fawredd, anweledig Dduw,
     Pa beth yw Dyn? – Pryd ddaeth Diddymdra'n fyw?

Ti Awdur Bywyd ers cyn tragwyddoldeb
  A ragfesuraist gorff ac enaid Dyn,
I'w ddodi'n Ben – echrydus gyfrifoldeb! –
  Ar ddarn o'th Gread yn dy le dy hun.
     O'th fod dy hun, Ffynhonnell pob peth byw,
     Fe'i tynnwyd ef; – hiliogaeth ddwyfol yw.

O gadarn Grëwr, rhyfedd yw dy lwybrau! –
  Er gweld o bell ei grwydro ef i gyd,
Rhoddaist wreichionen Bywyd yn ei lwynau,
  Fel y caet epil hyd eithafoedd byd.
     Â nerth y law, Grochenydd pridd di-liw,
     Do, ffurfiaist Ddyn; – a'i wneuthur megis duw.

Ti'r hollol-arall, heb dy weld, fawrygwn,
  Am roi ohonot ynom ryfedd rym;
Ninnau dy blant o'th flaen yn grwm a blygwn:
  Peraist in fod, a ninnau gynnau'n ddim.
     O flaen dy Wyddfod, holl-bresennol Dduw,
     Pa beth a saif? – Pa beth a ddeil yn fyw?

Daw hwyrddydd oes – er llonydd ei ehediad –
Daw – er na welwn ni ond golau'r wawr.
O Eiliad chwim! Ar dy ddisymud rediad
Sibrwd 'rwyt beunydd, "Agosáu mai'r awr".
At droed dy Orsedd, Farnwr dynol-ryw,
Fe'n dygir oll ryw ddydd, bob enaid byw.

Cans yr awr honno, 'nhwyr ein holaf Heddiw,
Treiddiwn drwy'r Llen i'r Dirgel sydd tu draw:
Ni'n llwch o lwch, ein lludw rown i'r lludw,
Cyn gweld a'n herys: breuddwyd – ynteu braw.
Gerbron dy Frawdle, driphlyg sanctaidd Dduw,
Llawn gyfrif fydd o holl eneidiau'r byw.

(Ar dôn y Tad Laurence)

ASH WEDNESDAY

Father Almighty, King of all creation,
  Whose gentle nod bade constellations be,
Thou knowest how one cell held yet a nation,
  And how the Void was given eyes to see.

    Each living thing was fashioned by that Hand –
    And at the last before its Lord must stand

O! for the secret of the endless turning
  Of those great stars! – Lord, have they worlds like ours?
How didst Thou kindle their primæval burning?
  Tell me their age in æons, cycles, hours...

    Each living thing was fashioned by that Hand –
    And at the last before its Lord must stand.

There was a time – nay, ages without measure –
  When none on earth of me had ever thought:
All that I have is mine by thy good pleasure;
  How can I boast, or think that I am ought?

    Each living thing was fashioned by that Hand –
    And at the last before its Lord must stand.

Age after age, each twinkling star still flashes,
  Yet every flame must flicker and must die:
Dust unto dust, nay, ashes unto ashes,
  From earth once drawn, in earth again I'll lie.

    Each living thing was fashioned by that Hand –
    And at the last before its Lord must stand.

Lord, wilt Thou end in dust Life's tragic story?
  Canst Thou forget this dust's great sigh for Thee?
Nay! – Death is but the portal unto Glory –
  Freed from my chains, thy Smile at last I'll see.

    Praise for all life, free gift of that vast Hand!
    Lord, at its end before thy Throne I'll stand!

(This is dedicated to the memory of Maurice Bévenot, S.J., whose brother, Dom Laurence Bévenot, O.S.B., has since set it to music.)

Y GRAWYS

O ddeugain nydd, O ddeugain nos,
O ddeugain gwawr a hwyrnos dlos,
Wrth lenwi'r rhod â'ch peraidd hun,
A deimlwch wacter Mab y Dyn?

O oriau llethol, oriau hir,
O ddidrugaredd wybren glir,
Wrth bylu'r Cread oll â'ch gwin,
A gofiwch syched llym ei fin?

O Haul! O Haul! Traw, llosga, lladd!
Dos, berwa'i Waed i'r eithaf gradd.
Ar dân boed dyfnder Greddf ei hun;
Tyrd, temtia, temtia Fab y Dyn!

Na, gwrthyd Duwdod dila nwyd:
I'w luniaeth, gŵyr am arall fwyd:
Brathiadau chwant a'i awchus fin
Chwenychodd – do, dan ddyfnach rhin.

A thi, fudandod anial nos,
Ti fantell ddu farwolaeth, dos –
Gorchuddia'r blaned hon â'th hun:
Â'r sêr mae cymun Mab y Dyn.

Noswylia, Grist; daw eto'r wawr.
Encilia hyd nes dêl dy awr,
Ac yna, dan forthwylion Dyn,
Rho iddo'r Llaw rodd iddo lun.

(Tôn: *Audi, benigne Conditor*)

First Friday in Lent

O Forty Days! O forty nights!
O lonely, lonely desert heights!
Bear witness each recurring year
To what your Maker suffered here.

Eternal solitary God,
This Solitude thy feet have trod;
This sound of Silence reached thine ears –
Th'unchanging Silence of the years.

The taste of hunger changes not,
Nor hath the Fast his bite forgot,
Pain hurts as it e'er hurt of yore –
Man walks where Man hath walked before.

O Son of God, now son of Man,
O Light of Life, now lifeless, wan,
Walk on, walk on, in search of shade
From rays of light thy Light hath made.

With Lucifer await the night,
Yet seek no respite from this fight:
Escape without there here is none –
The war within within is won.

Nay, conquer, Christ, the tempter's power,
Serene, await his last dark hour,
And then, 'neath thine own weeping light,
Extinguish this star's blackest might.

(Melody: *Audi, benigne Conditor*)

Following Day

O Solitude! O Solitude!
O hell bathed in beatitude!
Encounter with Eternity,
With Truth, hard Truth, Reality!

A man is what he is with thee:
The well-made mask that others see
Here cracks; – the great Act takes to rout:
Upon this rack the truth will out

Alone! – 'tis life endured and known;
Alone! – 'tis Stamina full-grown;
Alone; – alone, alone, alone,
'Tis naked Man's lewd bareness shown.

O Silence, Silence, shout aloud
Above the noise of this thick crowd
Of thoughts unceasing pacing round
The hollows of thy hollow sound.

O Stillness! Make my spirit still;
O teeming Void, its void fulfil;
O Emptiness! O Emptiness!
Thou strange, strange friend of Loneliness!

Alone with thee I'm all alone –
Alone with Him who is alone...
Alone? – Nay; when I'm all alone,
'Tis then I'm least of all alone.

O blessèd, blessèd Solitude!
Thou sole, ah! sole, Beatitude!
Surrounded on all sides by thee,
I'm stranded... in Eternity.

(Melody: *Nunc Sancte nobis Spiritus*, solemn tone)

Dydd Gŵyl Ddewi

Ai dyma'r bryniau droediwyd gynt gan Ddewi?
  A glywid unwaith yma beraidd siant?
Am eiliad boed i leisiau'r oes ddistewi:
  Daw ar fy nghlyw ddiamser eiriau'n Sant.
    O Ddewi Sanctaidd, rhodiaist gynt ein tir;
    Drwy'r oesoedd deil i'th lais atseinio'n glir.

Perffaith ddistawrwydd ydoedd grym dy bregeth,
  Ympryd di-dor dy hoff feunyddiol fwyd;
Boddhad dy gorff oedd gwaedlyd gosbedigaeth,
  Rhyndod y môr ddiwallai d'olaf nwyd.
    O Ddewi Sant, sancteiddiaist hwn ein tir;
    Â'th chwys argreffaist d'enw'n erwau d'annwyl sir,

Dy ddwylo ddygai ôl dy waith diderfyn,
  Hoeliwyd dy lygaid ar femrynau'r Nef.
Cysegrwyd tannau d'wddf at fwynaidd erfyn,
  Clustiau oedd gennyt at bob cwyn a llef.
    O Ddewi Sant, llafuriaist gynt ein tir;
    Adwaenost bwysau'r haul a'n gaeaf hir.

Awdurdod Crist a glywid yn dy eiriau,
 Arwydd ei Groes ddymchwelai allu'r Fall;
O dan dy draed symudai cadarn greigiau,
 Bendith dy law oedd olau dydd i'r dall.
  O Ddewi Sant, pregethaist yn ein tir;
  Hiraetha heno'i bridd am sain y Gwir.

O ddydd i ddydd disgwylit wŷs dy Geidwad,
 Nos ar ôl nos noswylit am y wawr...
'Rôl canrif gron daeth sain angylaidd alwad –
 Mynwes y Tad yw mur dy gell yn awr.
  O Ddewi Sant, do, ceraist d'annwyl dir;
  Bendithia eto'i addfwyn erwau pur.

A wêl dy enaid weithiau'i hen orwelion?
 A gofia naws yr Allor, swyn y côr?...
O Gymru! Gwrando lef dy fud adfeilion:
 "Dos! Sathra, chwâl sancteiddiaf demlau'r Iôr!".
  O Ddewi Sant, gorweddi dan ein tir;
  Ond saif yn d'enw lais hen greigiau hir.

                              (Ar dôn Mam)

St David's day

*(Reliving the pilgrimage made to St David's
on this day in 1975)*

In ages past upon these unaged mountains
  Myriads of saints once toiled in silent prayer.
With joy their soul drank from Salvation's fountains –
  Joy in the Cross the flesh was giv'n to share.
    Scarred were the hands that tilled these hills and dales,
    O David, raise those hands once more o'er Wales.

At night their chant, like incense, rose to heaven;
  As Earth rolled on, these stars their vigil kept.
At morn their praise was heard – at noon, at even –
  When twilight failed their souls 'mid Angels slept.
    Sweet to thine ears these singing hills and dales;
    O David, hear the beating heart of Wales.

Thy voice was heard on these our ways and byways –
  For love of Man thy silence thou didst break:
This human heart sought healing then, as always –
  Man unto Man the Light of God must take.
    Well knew thy feet these rugged hills and dales;
    O David, tread once more the roads of Wales.

Thine eyes drank deeply of thy Country's beauty
  Each rolling plain spoke of the Fields on high...
Thy gentle voice, torn by its sacred duty,
  Sang at the Altar that the Lamb was nigh.
    Tears bathed the eyes that loved these hills and dales;
    O David, cast one last sweet glance at Wales.

O blessèd dawn that brought the Seraph's message!
  Time ceased in one small twinkling of an eye:
Those hundred years grew dim in that strange passage
  From pain to unknown realms of bliss for aye.
    Yet here remain unchanged thy once loved vales;
    In glory, David, think again on Wales.

                (Melody: my mother's composition)

Yn ystod distawrwydd y Grawys

Unigedd! O Unigedd llwyr!
D'unigrwydd di, a'th brofodd, ŵyr,
Cans cyffwrdd wnaeth â dyfnaf trwch
Diddymdra ei gysefin lwch.

Ie, ef ei hun yn wir w dyn
Pan fyddo'n unig wrtho'i hun:
Y mwgwd cain a wêl y byd
Â'n yfflon, gyda'i ffugio i gyd.

Unigedd! – estron, estron dir!
Unigedd! – oriau... oriau hir...
Unigedd! – rhwng dy bewar mur
'Does dianc mwy rhag cwmni'r Gwir.

Y gwaliau hyn ŷnt dystion mud,
Hwy gadwant gyfrinachau drud:
Pe rhoddid llais i un o'r rhain
Ceid araith gan bob trawst a maen.

A thi ddistawrwydd tawel pur
Sy'n diasbedain rhwng pob mur,
Tyrd, treiddia 'nghalon i â'th swyn,
Distewa hi â'th sisial mwyn.

Digyffro dy lonyddwch di;
Sain Tragwyddoldeb sy'n dy si,
Curiadau Amser glywaf 'nawr
Yn mesur hyd pob munud awr.

O Wacter! Gwacter! Ateb! Clyw!
Pa le mae 'Ngheidwad? P'le mae 'Nuw?
– "Tu fewn, tu fewn, heb sŵn na sain,
A glywaist fyth ryw lefain main...?"

O wynfydedig unig le!
Yr unig wynfyd is y ne':
Yr unig bryd nad unig yw
Yw pan fo dyn yn un â Duw.

(Ar dôn wreiddiol)

ONE HOUR YET

*(before taking the step of prostrating myself in community
to beg admission to the ranks of the Fathers)*

What lies ahead? – the oceans sigh –
What lies beyond this blue, blue sky
That melts into the bluer sea
Of far, far, far off Mystery?

Where dost thou guide, unguided Sea?
O vast Unknown! – Could I but see
What lies a little out of sight,
Just further than the furthest light...

What Morrow rises 'neath that crest?
What dawn moves on from east to west
Each hour o'er this fast-sleeping earth
That lies, worn by Night's sated mirth?

Tomorrow, what will be Today?
To mem'ry, what new Yesterday?
Unknown, yet foreknown Mystery,
Thou'rt writ in Future's History.

Discovery! O Grace! O Grace!
Fair Newness! Soon I'll see thy face
Unveiled by Time's receding shade,
Now 'twixt two Nows awhile delayed

Surprise! How sweet thy sudden name!
Adventure! Men have sung thy fame.
What lurks behind this unturned page,
What plot unstitched, unsolved by age?

... Such was it once, long, long ago.
Well I recall how used to flow
Dawn after dawn to eventide,
Each born some mystery to hide...

But now each one knows where it goes,
Horarium is all it knows:
Each like the last reflects the next
And duplicates till death one text.

... One more... one more... and yet again
One more more similar refrain
That echoes echoes of the Song
Of Agelessness whole ages long.

– And yet, is't all that can expect
These dawning rays that well reflect
Each yesterday's exhausted morn?
May they yet wear some hue unworn?

The pregnancy of this dark night
Doth labour 'neath new bursting light:
This yesterday that doth arise
Bears p'haps just one, one small, Surprise?

Loquere, Domine: audit servus tuus

Silentium! Silentium!
Sodalis dormientium
In clausula dulcedinis
Stillantis solitudinis.

Hic solus tecum sum
Cum Solo, qui Silentium,
Illudque sol*um*, inhabitat
Eiusque sonum resonat.

O Quies! fac quiescere
In dulci tuo pectore
Hoc pectus quod in strepitu
Quietem quærit sonitu.

O Absens! reple Vacuum!
Fons silens horum fluctuum
Qu*i* in aëre nunc tinniunt –
Audisne tu qui t*e* audiunt?

O Tacens! Tacens!
Inanitas! te capere
Me doc*e* ac hanc præsentiam,
Palpar*e*, ut nosc*am* Essentiam.

O tenebrose Radie!
Micantem hic quotidie
Te cerno – immo, sentio –
Velat*um* autem Silentio.

O vasta devastata Nox!
Minuta murmurata Vox!
Te roboantem in medio
Æternitatis audio.

Exigua Vox sibilans!
Antiqua Aurora rutilans!
En cæcus manum tuæ do
Dum solus mundi in ora sto.

O gutta ex mari Temporis,
Quæ "Vita" a nobis diceris,
Heia! in te mersus, auferor
In Orientem e quo orior.

Æterne Solitarie,
In sæculis invarie
Soliloquens cum æonibus,
Nos soli soli te audimus.

Nam Pax cum pace loquitur,
Inane solum implebitur:
Auditur raro in strenuis
Susurrus Auræ tenuis.

Resertus in hac cellula,
Deserta quasi in insula,
Abscondor in Abscondito
Ignotus – nisi Incognito.

Tacentem tacens sentio
Hic solus cum Silentio
Beatæ Solitudinis –
Solæ Beatitudinis.

Nam sol*um* in solitudine,
Umbrante multitudine
Alar*um* invisibilium,
Non solu, nam cum Solo, sum.

(Melodia: *Mysterium Ecclesiæ*)

Ar ôl y Cymun

O! dyma ras! O! dyma ras,
Dyfnach na'r eigion eang las.
Llifo mae'i ddyfroedd oddi fry:
Gorlif y Nef yn nefoedd dry.
Ton ar ôl ton o'r nerthol fôr
A'm gylch bob awry n nilyw'r Iôr.

Gras yw ffynhonnell Bywyd clir,
Gras ydyw gwlith yr anial dir;
Gras, gras a wna i'r meirw fyw,
A Gras dry feidrol ddyn yn dduw.
Gras! Rhodder Gras! – heb ball na thrai;
Llif, Hylif mwyn, heb fyth leihau.

Gras, dim ond Gras, a'm lleinw i;
Syched am Ras yw 'nyfnaf gri.
Mesur difesur Rhodd y Nef
Chwalo argaeau'r Afon gref.
Digon yw hwn! Digonedd yw.
Diwedd ni ddaw – ni dderfydd Duw.

(Tôn: *St Catherine*, 125)

BENEDICITE

(ar doriad gwawr Sul yn y Grawys)

Llewyrch, O dragwyddol Wawr,
Cusana'n daear eto'n awr
Â chyntaf bendith † newydd ddydd,
Cynhaliaeth rhyw ddyfodol cudd.

GRÂCES

Rhown ddiolch, O Newydd-dra pur,
Am newydd fwynder ffrwyth a fflur,
Newydd-der, newydd gyfle'n dwyn
Newyddion na ŵyr eto'i swyn.

(Tôn: *Iam lucis orto sidere*)

BENEDICITE
(ganol dydd)

Bendithia †, O fendigaid Law,
Bendithia'r fendith hon a ddaw
O eigion dy fendithion gwyn
At wae'r melltigedigion hyn.

GRÂCES

Boed moliant it, Ffynhonnell Bod,
Am drefn y Drefn a drefna'r Rhod,
Y faith Ragluniaeth luniodd nwyd,
Liniarodd ef â lluniaeth bwyd.

(Tôn: *Rector potens, verax Deus*)

Melltigedigion...: cyfeiriad at y felltith a roed ar ddaear a roddai ei
ffrwyth megis o'i hanfodd.

BENEDICITE

(fin nos)

O dyner Olau, cyn it ffoi,
Rho olaf fendith † wrth in droi
Yn ôl, yn ôl i'r Nos lle bu
I ryw belydrau'n galw ni.

GRÂCES

Cwyd, gwmwl thus; cwyd, aberth mawl,
Ymdodda fry 'ngwaed cysglyd wawl
Y machlud sydd yn gwawrio draw
Dan fôr y Fendith gudd a ddaw.

(Tôn: *O lux beata*)

At Night
(mid-Lent)

When I'm alone, away from all that bustles,
Far, far away from all that howls and hustles,
When round mine ears the sound of Silence rustles –
    Then am I human.

O! *HAPPINESS*, unfold thy sacred letters.
What is the key that loosens man-made fetters?
Is't not to know what matters not, what matters,
    On one short journey?

Lord, I believe. Nay, Faith, this is my being.
Earth rolls and rolls, t'wards old Nirvana fleeing:
Born of a Star, my native starlight seeing,
    Homeward I travel.

Child of a day, and yet than daylight older,
Made to behold the eye of Time's Beholder,
Holding within Eternity's Upholder,
    Starward I wander.

Deeper and deeper, into deep'ning Presence,
Inward I swim, t'ward inward, inward Essence,
Holding the hand of that familiar Absence,
    Cast on some ocean.

Am I alone when in the hours of darkness
These eyes I shut and gaze into the blankness,
When eye meets eye, and looks upon Love's fairness,
    Hid in the Hidden?

                (Melody: *Ut queant laxis* / *Iste Confessor*)

IMMÉDIATEMENT APRÈS LE VOTE

"Admis!" dit-il, juste un seul mot,
La clef qui m'ouvre ton cachot...
Admis... Seignuer, à quoi? À quoi?
À l'Inconnu, connu de Toi.

* * *

Third Sunday in Lent

Days are passed in sorrow and joy.
Each little pain that doth annoy,
Each aching pleasure that must cloy
      Calls on, calls on.

Hours distil, fresh moments are spent;
Each *tick* unnotched is Being lent,
For each new breath from Heav'n yet sent
      Calls on, calls on.

Night! O Night! Thou buriest me
'Neath one short hour's tranquillity
Ere th'engines of Eternity
      Call on, call on.

(*Here begins retreat.*)

Lord, once more I lie at thy feet,
Here once again we pause to meet
Deep in Thy Heart, whose gentle beat
      Calls on, calls on.

One more year has borne me along
From prayer to prayer, from song to song
'Neath this great Bell, whose hourly gong
      Calls on, calls on.

Yet this Lent is not as the rest;
Nay, this retreat is one great quest
For what vocation richly blest
    Calls on, calls on.

Now, e'en now, two ways are to part:
Here all doth end, or all doth start...
New Manhood's strange relentless smart
    Calls on, calls on.

Youth is grown, its raiment now worn.
Fairness is marred, its last roots shorn.
O Plenitude! What years unborn
    Call on, call on?

Life! O Life! Thou liest ahead.
Life-history, thou'rt yet unread...
Aged fruitlessness, unknown, unwed
    Calls on, calls on.

Lord, is't all? Or can there be more?
Thou, Thou alone dost hold the door
Of Providence, whose teeming store
    Calls on, calls on.

Mystery! How rightly thou'rt named!
Veiled Destiny! In vain thou'rt tamed.
Who knows? Who knows what Plan unframed
    Calls, calls, calls on.

        (On original melody)

DECHRAU'R ENCILIAD

Daeth heno'r awr
I orffwys yn dy gôl,
I roddi heibio lyfrau gwaith,
Ffarwelio â'r holl ddaear faith
A mynd yn ôl.

Dwys ydyw'r awr:
Nid oes ond Ti dy hun
A minnau yma yn y gell;
Am wythnos gron fe gilia 'mhell
Holl leisiau dyn.

Ar freichiau'r Grog
'Rwyt yma'n awr o'm blaen:
Gorweddaf wrth dy ddrylliog draed
Â ffrwd dy bur faddeuol waed
Dros bob rhyw 'staen.

Crist! O! fy Nghrist,
Dy bresenoldeb di
Sy'n llenwi'r dwfn ddistawrwydd hwn,
Ac, er na'th welaf di, mi wn
Y'm gweli i.

Yn nyfnder hwn
Boed imi ddod o hyd
I gannwyll fwyn dy lygad di
Yn cwrdd â llygad f'enaid i
Mewn cariad mud.

Boed imi weld
Y pethau weli di
Yn nhemel sanct y galon hon
Nad ydynt deilwng ger dy fron
O'th Ysbryd cu.

Edrych yn ôl
I'r trist orffennol fu
A ddysg pa beth y dylwn wneud,
Pa beth o hyn ymlaen ei ddweud
Dan d'olwg di.

A phan ddêl pen
Y bur eiliadau main,
Gad imi ddychwel at fy ngwaith
Yn gyfoethocach dyn gan faeth
Y Sŵn di-sain.

(Tôn: *Laurence*, 28 yn y
Casgliad o Emynau Catholig)

BEGINNING OF RETREAT

Time, time again
Have I knelt here before,
Yet in this quiet eventide
I sense a Presence at my side,
    And I adore.

This is the night
On which I turn aside
From all that is not Thee alone
And tread into the great Unknown
    That Thee doth hide.

O! sacred peace
That bathes that blessèd Face!
Come, enter this my troubled breast;
In this retreat teach me to rest
    On gentle Grace.

Far, far away
Be all terrestrial noise...
The rowdy boast, the hollow word
Draw me no more: my soul hath heard
    The still, small voice.

For, Lord, we're two
In this Carthusian cell.
I *come apart to rest awhile*
Alone upon this desert isle
    'Twixt heav'n and hell.

    (*3.30 a.m.*)

When I look back
On all that hath gone by:
The days and hours that I have passed...
The memories that still cling fast –
    I weep, I cry.

Nay, nay, ne'er more
May I again recall
The opportunities of love,
The grace once given from above
    That I let fall.

Once, only once,
Is every grace bestowed.
Each hour of joy once lent to me
Unique in all eternity
    Hath onward flowed.

Now, only now,
Can I still order Time.
The Present is the Future's seed,
And men these present lines will read
    Of passing rhyme.

    Passage of Time!
This slowly-marching bell
Calls me to sleep and rest awhile...
Ring on, great Bell! – till Time thee style
    My passing knell.

> (Melody: *Laurence*, 28 in the
> Collection of Welsh Catholic Hymns)

En retraite

Dydd i ddydd a'm dwg at y Dydd,
Nos ar ôl nos i'r Ddunos fydd
Ryw ddydd, ryw nos yn wobr Ffydd
 Tu draw, tu draw.

Awr i awr a'm llusg yn fy mlaen
Wawr ar ôl gwawr, heb sŵn na sain
Ond adlef bell rhyw Alwad fain
 Tu draw, tu draw.

Eiliad ffug! A wyt ti yn bod?
Ni wnei ond dod, ail-ddod, ail-ddod...
Ac amgylchynu cylchau'r Rhod
 Tu draw, tu draw.

Amser! Sut dy ddiffinio di?
Ai cywir ein mesurau ni?
Ai ti sy'n cloi'r tragwyddol Si
 Tu draw, tu draw?

Blwyddyn arall lithrodd yn ôl
– Llithro? – Na, rhuthro'n wallgof, ffôl –
I'r fan lle'r oedd: i'th dawel gôl
 Tu draw tu draw.

Unwaith eto oedi a wnaf
'Rôl gaeaf arall, arall haf
Ennyd, er gweld i ba le'r af
    Tu draw, tu draw.

Oedi... ie, gafael yn dyn
Yn rhith y ffug eiliadau hyn
Sy'n toddi draw 'munudau syn
    Y Ddunos ddaw.

(Ar dôn wreiddiol)

En retraite: *LECTIO DIVINA*

Dan olau'r gannwyll hon
Craffaf ar eiriau'r nef;
Pwyso'r wyf heno ar dy fron
 Gan aros sain dy lef.

 Y geiriau sanctaidd hyn
 Yfaf un ac un:
Dan fud batrymau du a gwyn
 Llechu mae'r Gair ei hun.

Ysbryd gwirionedd pur
Fu'n cyfarwyddo'r pin
A grafodd ffurf llythrennau cu'r
Hen Roeg femrynau hyn.

Chwyth eto, Ysbryd Glân,
Ar y ffugurau hyn
Ac oddi ar y ffurfiau mân
 Llen y dirgelwch tyn.

Symud ar wyneb rhain
Fel dros yr Allor fry:
A'r trawsylweddiad cudd, di-sain
 Hylif yn Dduwdod dry.

Canys y syml ddŵr
A luniai'r marciau mud
A droes, yn nerth y wyrth ddi-stŵr,
Yn wirfod Gair i'r byd.

Yn yr anialwch gynt
Y cyfansoddwyd rhain:
Llefast drwy'r storm, drwy'r tân, drwy'r gwynt,
A thrwy'r llais distaw main.

Distaw yn wir yw'r awr,
A'r nos yn ddofn ei si:
Tyrd, tyrd yn agos, sibrwd 'nawr
Ryw air na wyddwn i.

(Tôn: *Bod Alwyn*, 5)

Dom Siméon
(Post ultimam acroasin in noviciatu)

O Bonitas! O Bonitas!
Dulcissima humilitas!
Israëlit*am* invenimus
In qu*o* incarnatus Dominus.

* * *

LINES SCRIBBLED IN RETREAT
(and left in their crudest form)

The voice of the past

You are too late, the master said,
 And drew upon his pipe...
– Oh! for one happy school-day, Lord!
 They're gone... I've grown... I'm ripe.

You are too late..., he puffed away,
 You'll have to wait a year.
– *A year? No! No, that is too long.*
 It must be settled here.

And so it was, unwisely, fast:
 I took a second best.
I let it slip between my hands,
 A grace, unique, thrice-blest.

The voice of the present

You are too late..., it rings again,
The phrase that kindly master said,
Who earlier had urged and urged
To dull, doped ears, duped, deaf, nay, dead.

Too late! Too late! – I'm cracking, Lord.
My heart swells up and heaves again.
Am I where Thou wilt have me, Lord?
Or am I labouring in vain?

How can I know? What should I do?
O Silent One! Thou, Thou alone
Must speak in this unending night
Ere't be too late, make, *MAKE IT KNOWN!*

(The Ampleforth, Blackfriars, Jesuit temptation has always
loomed large – together with their Oxford houses.)

In retreat

O! blessèd Cell, so quiet and so lonely,
Yet ever speaking to my crowded heart,
Stark are thy walls, thy windows – yet, so homely!
Suffered, endured, yet loved, is this strange hearth.

Known, so well-known, is every stone that holds thee
To these mine eyes, as unto theirs of old
Who studied, prayed, slept, laboured here before me
In this same stifling heat and aching cold.

Thou art the same; the number only changeth
On this small chart that hangs upon the wall.
This ancient Rule my life, like theirs, arrangeth;
Year after year this same great Bell doth call.

Known was the stillness of these sacred moments
That seem to freeze the very march of Time
To all who tasted Solitude's sweet torments,
Who bent their wills to this relentless chime.

Nay, Lord, I hear the sounds of joy, of sorrow
Coming across the barrier of the years:
Here, here they were, I am, they'll be tomorrow –
Their distant singing steals upon mine ears:

"...Walk on, our brother, tread where we have trodden.
O! blessèd penance that such glory wins!
Those sombre walls guard Paradise the golden.
Time ends... Today eternity begins."

(Melody: Rhys, 433)

O! blessed penance that has merited such glorious reward: echo of the words pronounced by St Peter of Alcàntara to St Teresa of Avila during an apparition.

Lectio Divina
(in retreat)

Here in my hands I hold
The Word that holdeth me;
These leaves I turn my self unfold
Writ, I am read of thee.

This same primæval Word,
That whispers now to me,
Cried, and by unmade Time was heard,
Spoke, and bade æons be.

In the eternal peace
Of unengendered Void
Truth thought aloud and bade Silence cease,
And with its echo toyed.

Verb of unceasing Act,
Logos of triune Thought,
Thy quiet *Fiat* uttered Fact,
Dreamt, and its dream-world wrought.

Star upon endless star,
Light on unending light,
Heard; – and, as summoned from afar,
Marched through th'eternal Night.

Be, thought the Poet's Mind;
    Am, was the Clay's reply...
– *Thou, Adam, shalt become Mankind.*
    Earth! with his will comply.

And Thou didst speak to me
    Deep in my mother's womb...
Nay, and again shall I yet hear Thee,
    Echo of uttered doom.

Deep is the Silence, Lord,
    The Silence of the years.
Lord! But a word, just one small word!
    Speak! for thy servant hears.

(Melody: *Bod Alwyn*, 5)

24TH OF MARCH
(Lines scribbled during collation)

I walk alone into the dark
That shrouds the hiddenness to come.
Noviciate! Familiar sound!
Ne'er more may I thee call my home.

This is the night that rules all nights,
The bridge 'twixt cowl and laity,
The dark that can beget a race
Or seal Potentiality.

Twelve hours to freedom – or to death
On Solitude's slow-writhing rack...
A choice, a word – nay, but a nod
Draws onward, or for e'er pulls back.

And in this choice all choices rest.
Each *possible* hangs on one whim.
To preach... to teach... to write... to be
Whatever else therein grows dim...

... Nay, or begins. O choice! O choice!
A life to live, a heart to love,
A brain that is not fully gleaned...
Yes, Lord, and Thee, my Judge above.

This life is short – as is the time
That separates my first retreat
From this my last in novicehood.
Whate'er its form, 'twill graveward fleet.

Good Lord, what else is there in life
Besides the *possibility* of grace,
The chance to gain new merit, ere
Be fixed for aye our heav'nly place?

What better use can here be made
Of this the sole, yes, sole new chance
Of doing what one day the soul
Will see in one last hurried glance:

– Ere for all time it says *Goodbye* –
As I this night, Noviciate –
To all that is not Thee alone,
My Lord, my God, my written Fate?

Y PUMED AR HUGAIN O FAWRTH

Beth glywaist ti, Forwynig fân?
Pa wefr gadd dyfnder d'enaid glân
Pan dorrodd drwy'r distawrwydd, gân
    O ryw gyfandir pell?

Pa beth a deimlaist, ddiwair Fron?
Ai ofn? Ai hedd? Ai ysgryd llon? –
Pan ddaeth drwy'r gwagle'r frawddeg hon:
    Freintiedig! Henffych well!?

Paham yr oedaist, wylaidd un?
Ai er parhau hyd angau'n fun –
Er gwaetha'r clod i ti dy hun
    Yn sain yr *Henffych well!*?

O fraint! O fraint! Anhygoel fraint!
Sut fedrit beidio â gweld ei maint?
At bwy o'r engyl, bwy o'r saint,
 Y bu'r fath *Henffych well!*?

Ond derbyn wnaethost – diolch byth! –
A chyda'th *Fiat* darfu'n syth
I'r *Fiat* cyntaf ddod i'n plith
    Dan atsain *Henffych well!*.

Y *Boed* a fu. Gwneuthurwr wnaed.
Er gwisgo'r cnawd a greodd, rhaid
Oedd gofyn rhodd dy gorff a'th waed –
    Oll dan un *Henffych well!*.

Dy *Fiat* drodd yn *Fuit* – do,
Yn hanes pob rhyw oes a fo,
A fu, a fydd, hyd fethiant co'
    Ar ryw gyfandir pell.

1982

(Ar dôn wreiddiol)

25TH OF MARCH

Is this the sound that thou didst hear
Long, long ago when thou wast here,
When that strange messenger drew near,
And said, *Hail, little maid!* ?

... The hush of this becalmèd night,
The darkness of Prayer's fastened sight,
The warmth of this angelic light
That whispered, *Hail, sweet maid!*...

– Canst hear again the rustling sound
Of Life fast sleeping on the ground
To which a while those feet were bound
That heard, *Hail, little maid!* ?

And tell me, gentle maiden dear,
This Song of Silence that I hear,
Hath it much changed since in thine ear
  'Twas broke by: *Hail, sweet maid!* ?

This spinning world, hath it much moved?
The march of Time, hath it improved
Th'eternal Peace that those ears loved
That heard, *Hail, little maid!* ?

And where thou art, sweet maid, this night,
Far, far away, hard by that Light
That hailed thee, is it silent quite?
— Dost hear each *Ave* prayed?

(On original tune)

Y PUMED AR HUGAIN O FAWRTH, 3.45 A.M.

Y noson hon 'rwy'n canu'n iach i'r byd,
Gan gloi am byth ffynhonnell ienctid gwyn.
Ffarwelio'r wyf â llu atgofion drud
Fy nefol uffern rhwng y muriau hyn:
Y *cariad cyntaf* wybu calon llanc
Wrth gymryd ar ei gefn d'arfogaeth Di,
Y weledigaeth ar y Wedd ddi-dranc
Gymerai le ei hanferth wacter hi...
O dirion Gell! Ti fuost ffyddlon im,
A minnau'n ffyddlon it drwy'r oriau maith.
Ti lyncaist fy ieuenctid megis dim –
Yr hogyn oedd i ebargofiant aeth...
Ffarwél, Nofisiaeth las! Ffarwél! Ffarwél!
Yn lifrai'r Nef af 'mlaen i'r oes a ddêl.

1982

143

11 A.M.
(25th of March)

The die is cast! O Rubicon,
Thou'rt crossed. Henceforth I must go on.
What might have been ne'er more may be.
O Cross! Now am I nailed to thee.

In two years' time 'twill be too late
To rearrange my earthly fate.
Now, now, e'en now the choice is made.
Short vow! On thee one life is weighed.

Farewell, fair Benedictine dreams!
Farewell, high academic gleams
Of glory gained in Campion Hall
Or in that studious Blackfriar stall!

Farewell, unborn, unknown new life!
And thee, unwed, ne'er made a wife,
Thee too, sweet Land, that ne'er shalt hear
The sermons ruminated here.

Nay, and to thee, green Novicehood
That taught me how to bear the Rood,
That witnessed every little pain
And joy that ne'er shall come again.

For on this day I leave behind
My youth, my past – as onward grind
The mills of slow-maturing age:
This little vow is one huge stage.

Chartreuse! I now belong to thee.
Thou knowest what thou'lt hold for me
From day to day to that last day
When these short days grow dim for aye...

– And cede their place to one more stage
Already crossed by age on age
Of holy brethren dressed like me
Who marched this way to victory.

O grace! O grace! How could I doubt?
Old Satan! Now thou'rt put to rout
By these three words that crossed the lips
Of one that from thy claws now slips.

O David! Bruno! On I come.
This Charterhouse shall be my home
Till ye shall deem it well to hail
And draw from these small hands each nail...

– And open wide some unknown Door
That none shall close, e'er, evermore,
And say, *Behold what's laid for thee,*
With us, till fades eternity!

Y LLYFR GWEDDI

Arwyddaf heddiw ddalen bitw, fân
Arwyddwyddwyd ganrif gron yn ôl gan un
A ddaliai'r llyfryn hwn fel fi'n ei chân
Tra eto 'nghyntaf lesni diwair fun
Yn llawn breuddwydion am ddyfodol pell
Gysegrai ar y bore hapus hwn,
Wrth dyngu, fel myfi, byw'r Bywyd Gwell –
Heb weld y ddoe'r yfory heddiw wn...
O dyner wyry ieuanc, hen Hen Nain,
Ti roist im heddiw neges glywais gynt,
Ond byth erioed â'r cyfryw eglur sain,
Cans tybiais glywed gân dy Ddoe'n y gwynt:
"Trosglwyddo wneuthum ffagl y rhawd i ti.
Fe'i deliais awr... Gwna dithau fel myfi."

1982
(ganrif yn ddiweddarach)

THE PRAYER BOOK

This night I sign a little, little book
Here signed in this same year by one small hand
One century ago, as it too took
A pledge to journey on toward the land
Of which at sweet fifteen it little thought –
Not knowing what strange motherhood did wait
To turn the Beauty that I saw to nought
And interrupt for e'er one pregnant fate.
Fair eyes! I looked and looked, and looked again
Into the distance into which these gazed...
Plucked flow'r! Thy tiny womb maintained the chain
Intact, that for an hour extinction grazed.
O little hand! Thou'rt linked on this small page
To one loose end that ends Eve's endless age.

PROMITTO

Nid arswyd Uffern dân a'm tyn i ffwrdd
O'r hyn yr wyf, o'r hyn a'm gwnaeth yn ddyn,
Na gobaith pell am ryw amheuthun fwrdd
Gymero le ryw ddydd y dorth ddi-lun,
Na 'chwaith yr awydd am wneud rhywbeth gwell
Nag eraill, ar y siwrnai hon sy'n rhan
I bawb sy'n ymdaith tua'r Ganaan bell,
A'm cloi'n y cyfryw ryfedd, ryfedd fan –
Ond Person; – un gymerodd fy holl fryd
O'm cwffio'n sydyn ar fy nhalcen hyf;
Rhyw Gyfeillgarwch, mor anhygoel ddrud,
Ddatblgodd yma hyd nes dod mor gryf
Â thagu pob rhyw gariad fedrai fod,
Ond cariad at y Cariad sy'n troi'r Rhod.

1982

RENOUVELLEMENT DES VŒUX

'Tis not the fear of Hell that moves my soul
To seek the Face that sought me ere I breathed,
Nay, nor the sight of those great clouds that roll
Across the vault of Heav'n, with glory wreathed,
That bid leave now behind whatever moves
Outside the orbit of one tiny cell,
And clip the wings of unfledged angel loves,
And throw away the key of this strange hell...
But someone that I met long, long ago
When yet unwarned of what this stranger did
To those who, unawares, did near him go,
Unarmed against his slow, sly, cunning bid:
"Wilt give me this... and this... yes, p'haps and this?
This too?... p'haps this as well... in turn for bliss?"

Jam jacta est alea! Heu! nunc
Migratus sum in locum hunc
In quo introducti pereunt
In Oculo quem fugiunt.

AFTER ANOTHER ACCIDENT
(as excitateur)

O precious boon! unknown save unto those
Who know thee not, whom seeking, none may find,
The moment of whose coming no one knows,
For if he did, he'd hold it yet behind
A little longer, till at last no more
He could thee see... Lo me once more this night
Alone with this thine absence, on the shore
Of all that lies 'neath this world's fastened sight...
– Aha! Aha! Thou caught'st me off my guard!
The matin bell is ringing. 'Tis full morn!
'Tis true! Raves cease thy raving to retard.
I know thee only when from thee I'm torn.
O Sleep! Hadst not come of thine own accord,
From first to last this day thou'dst been my lord.

Accident: Community once more woken two hours too soon.
(Doubly unpopular: hour brought forward yesterday, hence only
five hours' sleep.)

MEMORIES THAT LINGER

"What are you?" said the little head
That touched the head on which it leaned,
When I held Childhood on my back,
Myself from childhood barely weaned.

"Are you a boy? Are you a man?
Which is it? Tell me, tell me, please!"
"Aha!" laughed I, "Well may you ask,"
Amazed at how e'en infants tease.

We walked a little further on,
And I remember how I thought
How sweet it was to be embraced
By Innocence unsoiled, untaught.

Without a word we reached the tree,
And lo! – as only children can –
"No, tell me please!" she carried on,
"Which is it? Which? A boy or man?"

"Let's say somewhere between the two,"
I said, and hoped that that would do;
Then walked a little further on
While she thought hard upon the clue.

And yet again the question came:
"Why won't you tell me which is true?
Please tell me. Please!" – and, ta'en aback,
I 'gan to wonder what she knew.

"I'm half a boy, and half a man"
Was all my tortured brain could find,
And, swooning gently on my head,
She turned the words in her strange mind...

O Childhood! Art thou rightly named
With thoughts so deep in heads so small?
And thou, sweet load, where art thou now?
Should I thee "Girl" or "Woman" call?

Memories: I.S.C.F. Camp, Harrow,
1970

AR DDECHRAU PYTHEFNOS Y DISTAWRWYDD MAWR

Pan gano'r gloch sy'n selio oriau'r t'wyllwch
Dan allwedd haearn Rheol y Tawelwch,
Pan suddo'r byd i lewyg pur drythyllwch,
    A wyf yn unig?

Pan huno'r Clas dan haen hen ebargofiant,
Pan gysgo'r Oes tan fantell tawel fwyniant,
Pan roddo Nos i firi Sain fyr Seibiant,
    A oes distawrwdd?

A phan ddiffoddwyf lachar gri'r goleuni,
A throi fy nghlust at furmur dudew'r meini,
Pan deimlwyf adain Hedd droso' i'n ymdaenu,
    A yw hi'n dywyll?

A phan edrwychwyf i ddyfnderau'r Gwacter,
I ymysgaroedd hanfod yr Ehangder,
Pan deimlwyf bwysau llethol fy mychander,
    A oes Diddymdra?

Wrth gau f'amrannau 'nghôl dy ddiwair heddwch,
O ddyfnder Nos, a gwrando su Llonyddwch,
Teithiaf i mewn at gyfrin graidd Dedwyddwch
    Tu hwnt i'r dyfnder.

Tcithiaf i berfedd dyfnaf y distawrwydd,
Yn nhawch y caddug teimlaf am ryw arwydd...
O! estron dir – ac eto mor gyfarwydd
    Cwmni Unigedd!

(Tôn: *Ut queant laxis* / *Iste Confessor*)

THINKING ALOUD
(after seeing picture of Llanfyllin on calendar for month of April)

There'll never be another chance.
O Lord, you gave me one, but one.
I took it, Lord; I used it, Lord;
Abused, misused it; now it's gone

For ever and for evermore.
The clock marks once throughout all time
Each drop of Presentness that falls
Between each instantaneous chime...

Before it joins the company
Of others that can be no more.
It matters little what the space
'Twixt this one and the one before:

Once it has trickled through my hands
And crossed the frontier of the Now,
It is as far from human grasp
As any that I've known or know.

The irretrievable has gone,
And goes each moment further off.
This last does but begin its flight:
To launch it, one small tick's enough.

Goodbye, poor, uncorrected Past!
Goodbye, unfelt, unvalued Youth!
Could I but have you back one day
Within my hands, now that the Truth

Has taught me what is meant by Grace –
That is, the meaning of a Gift –
What is the value of a choice,
The art of knowing how to sift

Importance from its brother, Air,
Worthwhileness from its sister, Noise,
And how, how precious is one hour
That in the Here and Now does poise

My wobbling soul 'twixt what may be
And what, if 'tis, must be ruled out
For ever, ever, evermore
By Fate that from all time does shout:

"Take care, take care, child of an hour:
Reflect before you burn its oil.
I give it once, once only. Hear?
One tick Eternity can spoil."

LINES WRITTEN ON FEAST OF THE COMPASSION OF THE BLESSED VIRGIN

I write in vain. I write in vain, in vain.
'Twere better not to take my eyes from Thee,
Good Lord, and do as doth the Rule ordain
That bids full peace vain correspondence flee.
None e'er shall see this sentence that I write;
This page, like me, will end its life in dust:
Through life, through death, removed from human sight,
The hermit and his scribblings vanish must.
And yet, is't vain the message that a friend
Writes to his friend, e'en should the latter know
Each syllable from aye, ere he aught send
As Thou, Lord, this small *WORD* readst oft ere now.
For Thee alone I write, my Lord... My Lord,
For Thee alone shall burn each unread word.

Retraite mensuelle

I came across an envelope one day
Among the sheets with which Carthusians speak,
And suddenly Monotony gave way
To bubbling Joy, as like a flash did streak
Across the screen of Memory a horde
Of utterly forgotten minutes spent
In Youth's fair prime, when word was put to word
To form the letter that in this was sent.
... *Le Maître des Novices,* read the first line...
And *France* had been left out – yet nonetheless,
The writing I beheld was really mine,
And Providence its journey deigned to bless...
And I recalled how thick the question mark
That hung o'er what I sent into the dark.

Envelope: Father Master had given us a number of used envelopes.
It is on the backs of these that we send notes to each other – out of
poverty. (The notes, however, have to pass through him.)

SUL Y BLODAU

Marchog bellach, Frenin Nef,
Trwy waedd Hosanna'r dyrfa gref:
Sain buddugoliaeth glywir 'nawr
Dros holl fyddinoedd Uffern fawr.

Â gwylaidd rwysg dos yn dy flaen
At ennaint poeredd, coron ddrain.
At orsedd syn tro dyllog draed,
Yn fantell deyrn gwisg rudd dy waed.

Dos rhagot, Grist; do, deaeh dy awr,
Nesaodd d'olaf frwydr fawr:
Yr oruchafiaeth sydd gerllaw;
Baneri'r Deyrnas welir draw.

Ymlaen! Ymlaen! Eneiniog Duw;
Ymlaen! Bendefig dynol-ryw:
Dy ganlyn di wna byddin gref
Drwy'r oesoedd ddêl hyd byrth y Nef.

Marchoga felly, D'wysog gwiw,
Trwy lyn dy waed i'n dwyn at Dduw.
Jerwsalem a'th erys di –
O'th Groes teyrnasa arni hi.

(Tôn: *Ride on, ride on in majesty*)

PALM SUNDAY
(after ceremony)

The time has come, O King of Kings,
To enter on thy princely power.
Already the Hosanna rings
As nearer draws thy regal hour.

The voice of earth, of sky, of sea
Now joins with ours, as we Thee hail
The Father of the world to be
Torn open by each royal nail.

March on, march on, O Victor, march
T'ward this strange throne prepared for Thee;
For one short hour bend 'neath this arch
That subjugates Eternity.

And then lift high that Head again
To see the light that doth await
Beyond the dark that felt thy pain:
Ride through Heav'n's newly opened gate.

(Melody: *Exsultet cœlum laudibus*, or: *Ride on, ride on in majesty*)

HAWL I GYFFWRDD

A yw'n wir fod syml rithiau'n
   Cuddio Crëwr, Barnwr Dyn?
A fydd pabell fechan hithau'n
   Do i'r Duwdod maith ei hun?
Llusern ffyddlon! A wyt tithau'n
   Gwarchod cwsg y Sanctaidd Un?

Credaf; credaf, er na welaf –
   Credaf air y Gwir ei hun:
Geiriau genau'r Sancteiddiolaf
   Ddoe a heddiw ŷnt yr un.
Hwn yn wir yw'r Swper Olaf:
   Amser Duw ni fesur Dyn.

Ef ddywedodd, Ef addawodd –
   Ie, hefyd Ef a wna.
Gair o'i enau wnaeth y bydoedd,
   Gair ei was ei rym ryddha.
Ef yng Nghana a orchmynnodd,
   Torth Berea ufuddha.

O ddirgelwch! O ddirgelwch!
  Doethion leisiau'r byd a chwardd.
Popeth yma sydd gyfarwydd,
  Eto yma popeth dardd.
Iaith dirgelwch yw distawrwydd –
  Harddwch Duw i Ffydd sydd hardd.

Felly boed! O ryfedd neithior!
  Credaf heb ymofyn pam.
Af ymlaen i'r Uchel Allor,
  Er y cryndod yn fy ngham.
Gwyn ei byd, y llaw a dorro'r
  Bara – nage,'r Oen di-nam!

(Tôn: *Tantum ergo Sacramentum*)

MAUNDY THURSDAY

When angels' little eyelids weep
    O'er what man doth to man,
Heav'n's smallest breasts feel chagrin deep,
    As only spirits can.

When suffering is felt in Bliss
    And ecstasy grows pale,
Rejoicing sings a note amiss,
    Th'eternal Sirens wail.

And when those little pupils peep
    Into the heart of Man,
Beatitude itself doth weep,
    Light's very light grows wan.

Good Lord, can we rejoice on earth
    When Heav'n itself doth cry?
How deep is this world's deepest mirth
    That in the next doth sigh?

The very song of Earth is sad,
    And sadder now that Heav'n
Is saddened o'er both good and bad
    That Good's own Heart have riv'n.

Can it be so, my dearest Lord?
      Is't possible? Is't true?
The very souls who hold thy Word
      Are damned by what they knew.

For on this day we eat Thee, Lord,
      And eating choose our fate:
This Particle can Bliss afford,
      Or shut for aye its gate.

'Tis thine own word, sweet Lord, good Lord,
      Confided to a friend:
"Of souls unwashed a filthy horde
      Among the just doth blend."

"The hatred of the Food of Love
      Hath grown too great, too great.
The very gates of Heaven move:
      Its blessings Hell now sate."

O Sadness! Deep thou art, how deep!
      Deep, deeper than the height
Of Tragedy, o'er which shall weep
      Marred æons' blurred, barred sight.

(Melody: an adaptation of a psalm melody learnt at La Trappe)

DYDD IAU CABLYD
(yn hwyr y dydd)

Ai dyma'r Bara dorrwyd gan ei ddwylo –
  Dwylo fy Ngheidwad, cyn eu rhwygo hwy?
Ai dyma'r Cwpan yfwyd gynt dan wylo
  Y noson honno cyn yr erchyll Glwy'?
Ai dyma'r Gwin a alwyd ganddo'n Waed,
  Ffrwyth y Winwydden sathrai'r byd dan Draed?

Oes ar ôl oes atseinio mae'i orchmyn:
  "Rhennwch, cymerwch, yfwch yn fy nghof."
Sant ar ôl sant fu'n dal y Cwpan Cymun;
  Minnau fel hwy at Neithior Cariad ddof.
Yn nhoriad hwn fe'hadnabuont Ef,
  Yn nafnau hwn dihidlai Neithdar Nef.

Gnweir, clywir eto acen y Lleferydd
  Yma lle'r wyf, dan Chwa'r Brif-Allor hon;
A'r Ymgyffyrddiad, arall eto'i gwybydd,
  Gras eto lifa,'n don ar dyner don:
Cans cwmni hwn yw cyfaneddiad Duw,
  A'r Gwacter hwn, Ymgyfarfyddiad yw.

Yfaf, bwytâf Fedd, Fara pur Angylion;
  Amser a mesur yma nid ŷnt mwy:
Clywaf a glywyd gynt gan Apostolion,
  Teimlaf a deimlodd eu calonnau hwy.
Un ydwyf i ag Undod yr holl Saint –
  Fendigaid Gymun! Di-ddydd, di-ddiwedd Fraint!

(Ar dôn Mam at emyn Dewi Sant)

MASS OF LAST SUPPER

Can it be that in this vessel
  All the Godhead meekly hides?
Doth He choose in thee to nestle
  Who the clouds of heaven rides?
Here doth Faith with Reason wrestle –
  'Neath this Tent all Truth abides.

Reason reigns in every quarter,
  Reason now can tame the stars,
Et in this will Reason falter –
  Lack of proof the theorem mars.
Faith, a simple maiden's daughter,
  Takes the leap that Reason bars.

"What is Faith?" here ponders Reason;
  "Common maid! I know her not.
Break my laws? 'Tis highest treason.
  Creeds against my kingdom plot."
Reign, great King; enjoy thy season.
  Faith would not exchange her lot.

Nay, she sees what thou wilt never
  See or feel or know at all.
Unlike thee, nor wise nor clever,
  She knows nought, her heart is small.
Nought, all nought, she hungers ever
  For a thought, a word, a call.

... Call me, Lord, my heart is broken.
　Speak! My pride is emptied, crushed.
From a dream as though awoken,
　This loud brain is strangely hushed.
All Man's words are best unspoken –
　Wind has ever howled and gushed.

Truth, speak on. Thy slave is list'ning.
　I'll devour each word I hear.
Nothing, utter, utter nothing –
　Such I am; the mask I tear.
Now I grasp Thee, God in hiding! –
　Faith! 'Tis Faith! 'Tis Vision clear!

(Melody: *Tantum ergo Sacramentum*)

Toriad gwawr, Gwener y Groglith

Fe wawria heddiw ryfedd ddydd,
Argaeau'r Nef sydd oll yn rhydd;
Cwyd yntau'r Haul o'i gwsg yn awr
I weld ymaflyd Nef a Llawr.

Ceriwbiaid a Seraffiaid Nef
Ostegant 'nawr eu sanctaidd lef;
Holl ymysgaroedd Natur sydd
Yn frwysg dan win yr estron ddydd.

Cans clywir heddiw oernad Oen
Yn suddo dan arteithiol boen:
Creawdwr cnawd trwy'i gnawd ei hun
Yn rhwygo'r llen rhwng Duw a Dyn.

Bur Ddwylo sanct a luniodd Ddyn,
Derbyniwch am oll ddiolch, wŷn
Ei gusan haearn. Dyllog Draed,
A droediodd don, rhowch don eich gwaed.

O henffych well, garedig Groes,
Ti unig obaith unig oes!
Sain buddugoliaeth glywir 'nawr:
Gorffennaist waith dy erchyll awr.

Ergydion cryf dy hoelion dur
Ddymchwelodd ragfur Gwynfyd pur.
Concweraist hen Goncwerwr Dyn –
Do, lladdwyd heddiw Angau'i hun.

O flaen dy draed, glwyfedig Dduw,
Ymgrymed 'nawr bob ysbryd byw:
Ti sethraist winwryf llid yr Iôr –
Dos rhagot! Sathra dir a môr!

(Tôn: *Vexilla Regis*)

At dawn
(Good Friday)

O dawn of dawns! O day of days!
How strange, how eerie seem thy rays!
The Light of lights thy light's own beams
This day will darken 'neath Hell's gleams.

For on this day such groans are heard
As numb the use of thought or word.
Re-echo, hills, the sound of pain:
A bleating lamb is torn and slain.

Walk on, O Christ, the end is nigh.
Stretch out thine arms, look to the sky;
Bathe in the Blood that sets us free,
In death nail Death to this strange Tree.

All hail, sweet Cross, our only hope!
Hail, every nail and beam and rope
That raised a Victim white and pure
O'er altar strange, th'estranged to lure.

Three hours of Hell Heav'n now hath proved,
All Satan's realm hath rocked and moved.
'TIS DONE! The veil is rent in twain.
Lo! fallen, fallen Hell's domain.

O Christ, thy piercèd feet have trod
The winepress of the wrath of God.
March on, O King, tread earth and sea!
Hold forth thy Sign of Victory!

(Melody: *Vexilla Regis*)

STAT CRUX DUM VOLVITUR ORBIS
Good Friday)

O Tree of Life, my Saviour's Cross,
Repair the Tree of Eden's loss;
Stretch forth thine arms o'er all mankind,
That wand'ring Adam shade may find

Victorious Tree, triumphant Tree,
The Universe lies under thee:
Unmoved thou standest o'er the world,
Unrocked, as this small globe is whirled.

Thou art the crux of all that is,
The hinge where hangs all that is His
And what is ours in time and space,
The universal meeting place.

Thou pointest upward to the skies,
Thou pointest to where Satan lies,
Thou reachest out to sea and land,
Thou holdest thy Creator's hand.

O Gibbet, thou shalt judge the world:
The echo of thy final word
Shall sound, resound from end to end
Of Space that doth for e'er extend.

(Melody: *Ride on, ride on in majesty*)

HOLY SATURDAY
(at dawn)

Where wast Thou, Christ, on this dark day,
So dark that none in church may pray,
That o'er the earth no Sacrifice
May be received in Paradise?

"My Lord they've ta'en away," I hear;
"Where have they laid my Treasure dear?"
The real Absence fills the Tent
O'er which this day no Wing is bent.

The very angel hosts have flown
From this their nest, and no more own
The Sacred sleeping 'neath their feet:
No lamp reflects their light and heat.

O Absence! O vast Emptiness!
How hollow this day's Loneliness!
No song, no office, not a face
To bring one tiny ray of Grace...

My solitude is absolute,
Nay, e'en my Friend doth seem so mute
That in this heart a something sighs
For gazing at these silent skies.

O Void! Where is my other Half?
O Angels! Shout on my behalf.
Bring back, bring back, bring back my Lord!
Bring but a drop of Grace, a word...

"On this dark day the Hidden One
Is hid e'en from the very sun
That He enkindled – nay, nay more,
Doth hide Himself, 'neath Mystery's Door.

"E'en we ourselves may penetrate
No further, for the very Gate
Of unrevealed, unknown full gloom
Is barred, and Doom awaits its doom.

"He's hid, we say, and hid He'll be
'Neath Hiddenness no eye may see –
Thine least of all, poor carnal soul!
Await, await... Let Fate unroll.

"All that we know is that full nought
Is all the knowledge ever sought
By little hominides like thee
Who know but half Eternity."

(On original melody)

EVENING OF SAME DAY

Ah! memories! How sweet they are –
And yet how painful to the heart
That sees each one as from afar
And reaches out lest it depart,
In vain, for part it must... it has...
It will... yet will again return
As sweet as at the first it was,
To rouse Pain's embers that still burn.

It hurts, good Lord, and yet I feel
Some little spark, deep, deep within,
Some faint, faint echo that doth steal
Across the grinding Past's loud din
On these calm eremitic ears
Now stabilized with frozen Time
That, station'ry, surveys the years
And freezes them anew in rhyme.

O inward sigh! Thou art repressed,
And yet thou'rt heard on Heaven's height...
"Who would have thought, who could have guessed – ?
A monk, him, *him*! E'er hid from sight!..."
Ah! such a childhood, protestant,
Impassioned, rowdy, impish, rude,
Epitome of Discontent
Content this night with crusts for food...

(5 p.m. as I write)

Grace! How thy ways are nebulous!
The clock strikes out the hour, the day
On which the most ridiculous
Came true, and brought a drummer gay
Upon his knees before a Saint
Who, though the rascal little knew,
Had traced for him in letters faint
A word that soon a heart would woo.

O Book of Life! Two columns bright
Are marked on these thy gilded leaves:
The one, writ in eternal Night,
Marked with the Plan that Wisdom weaves,
The other void, to be yet filled –
Though filled a little every hour –
With one short question: "Was't fulfilled?"
– And one last space: "Which of the Four?"

Heav'n waits, and so doth Purgatory;
One last faint hope in Limbo lies;
Hell sings Despair's invitatory,
And hides its music from our eyes...
O Lord, I dangled o'er the last:
Precocious sinner, had I left
My body in my putrid past,
My damnèd soul by Hell were cleft.

The hour that strikes struck then in time:
"And to this Church I pledge my life..."
From thence Thou bad'st me slowly climb,
From that abyss of graceless strife,
And, in the silence of that Saint,
Not as at first, 'mid brimstone show'rs,
But with a word, e'er, e'er so faint,
Thou mad'st it known to all my powers:

CARTHUSIAN was the graven word
Writ large, yet hard at first to read,
On that strange Book – and Thy steel sword
Did all the rest, e'en though I bled
Beneath the writhes that severed me
From what a growing heart could love
Too well – for it was made for Thee,
Thee, Thee alone, as't reads above.

Memories: of these minutes (between 5 and 6 p.m., 10th April, 1971) in St David's Chapel, Ampleforth.

NOSON Y PASG, **3.45** A.M.

Pan gofiwyf sut y'th gerais dithau gynt,
Fy Nuw, fy Mhriod, f'unig annwyl Un,
A gweld yn awr fy nhrychinebus hynt,
A chyflwr f'enaid llugoer, trist ei lun,
Daw arnaf awydd wylo dagrau twym
Dros bwll anobaith hollol-wastraff oes
Sydd er ei phenyd oll yn dal yn rhwym
At Hunan Fawr, gan ddal i ofni'r Groes.
Cans gwelaf nad wyf gam ymhellach 'nawr
Yn 'r Yrfa nag yr oeddwn ar y dydd
Yr wylais gan lawenydd oedd mor fawr
O gael nesáu at Ddirgeleddau'r Ffydd.
Y noson hon yr oedd, y noson hon!
Y noson hon daeth *Lumen Christi* i'm bron.

1982

The First day of the week

Despondency... despondency...
O what dejected company!
He's dead! He's dead! The Master's dead!
For three whole years vain hopes we've fed.

And yet we thought that it was he,
The Christ, the Jews' delivery,
The One that all the Books foretold –
For thirty silver pieces sold!

What next? How shall we spend our lives?
Shall we regain our work, our wives?
It's over. He is dead and gone.
We've lost. We've failed. The Jews have won.

And as for him who ate our bread –
How long had this been in his head?
He has it now, his heart's desire:
A place of honour in Hell fire.

Disperse, it's all we can do now.
Our hearts are at an all time low.
Things will work out. They'll brighten up.
Forget that Bread... Forget the Cup...

A world-wide church built by twelve men!
We must have been stark raving when
We put our trust in this strange man
From Nazareth! – that backward clan!

What hit me? Ouch! What's shining there?
Ow! Stop it! Stop that dazzling glare!
"It's Him!" – "It's not?" – "Yes, look! It's Him!"
"You're joking." – "No, it's not a whim..."

– "Shalom! Shalom! Hail, brethren, hail!
Doubt not. Behold where stood the nail.
'Tis I. I have o'ercome the world.
Go forth!... Convert it to my word."

NOS Y PASG

Distawrwydd perffaith heno sydd
Yn disgwyl, disgwyl toriad dydd:
Dan fantell eu mudandod oer
Noswylia'r bryniau 'ngolau'r lloer.

Hwy wyddant fod rhyw Olau'n dod,
Rhyw danbaid Wres yn rhuddo'r rhod;
Sylfeini eu cadernid hwy
Sy'n gwynio dan ryw enfawr glwy'.

Cynhyrfant... Crynant... – Beth sy'n bod?
Pa drydan saethodd 'nawr drwy'r rhod?
Pa fflach gynhyrfodd sêr y nen?
Beth dorrodd gwsg y lleuad wen?

Goleuni! Gwawl! Disgleirdeb Haul!
Y creigiau gwynant hyd eu sail.
Agorant! – methant gynnwys mwy
Egnïon eu carcharor hwy.

Cyfododd! – do, 'r tragwyddol Wawr;
Mae'n rhydd! Mae'n rhydd! Hon, hon yw'r Awr.
Gorchfygodd! – ie, 'r byd i gyd,
Mae'r oll dan ei lesmeiriol Hud.

Hwn ydyw'r Dydd! Hwn ydyw'r Dydd!
Dawns fawr y Cread ergyd rydd.
Y Wawr! Y Wawr! Y brydferth Wawr
A dorrodd – do, hyd gyrrau'r llawr.

(Tôn: *Rex sempiterne, Domine*)

SAIF Y GROG TRA Y TRY'R DDAEAR
(Llun y Pasg, 3.0 a.m.)

Beth ddaw yfory drwy riddfannau'r Gell?
Pa sain gyffyrdda'r clustiau tawel hyn
Ag adlef ysgafn o'r gorffennol pell
Sy'n dal i droi 'Mhresennol gwaraidd Ddyn
Tu draw, tu draw i chwi, gymrodyr mud
Sy'n cadw f'anghyfannedd annedd fân
Rhag golwg 'nôl at gu gomorraidd fyd,
Rhag hudol donfedd ei lesmeiriol gân?
Gyfarwydd furiau! Sefwch yn ddi-sain
Fel doe ac echdoe, fel drwy'r ganrif hon,
Ac fel drwy'r ganrif gynt a'r un o'r blaen
O gylch rhyw saint na chlywyd am eu sôn.
Mae'r byd yn dal i droi, tu draw, tu draw,
Ond yma try ar echel oriau ddaw.

1982
Llun y Pasg: Priodwyd Dad a Mam ar yr ŵyl hon, 1947.

184

EASTER MONDAY
(after Mass)

O Sadness! How the pain is deep!
We could not even vigil keep.
What we have sown we now but reap...
  – Quem quæritis?

Good Sir, if thou know'st ought of this,
Or canst explain what is amiss,
Pray, tell us where our Treasure is.
  – Quem quæritis?

Thou knowest well who 'tis we seek!
Jerusalem throughout this week
Hath known no other Master meek...
  – Quem quæritis?

We seek the One that Israel taught,
The One that we the people thought
Would bring these Occupants to nought...
  – Quem quæritis?

But Sir, thou surely must have heard
Of this great Name at least a word:
We seek the Lord, the *Lord*, the *LORD!*
  – Quem quæritis?

Thou dost, good Sir, but hurt us more.
The wounds we feel are yet too sore
To be thus spurned. We'll thee ignore,
     Quem quæritis.

Seek if ye wish, But why seek here?
Why seek a living in a bier? SURREXIT.
– What? – *Nay, thou didst hear.*
    You mean...? – *It is.*

               (On original melody)

Sunset of same day

Walk on, disciples, to the night
Grey-hearted as the evening light,
Your downcast eyes fix on the road,
Bent double 'neath your heavy load.

Look not up now – what could it do?
Nay think not e'en to question who
Is standing there – all, all alone,
A Stranger – yet, as 'twere well known.

Walk on with this man at your side.
'Tis dark'ning, slacken not your stride
Until that little town ye greet
Emmaus: there you'll rest your feet.

He cannot stay, he must go on –
Nay, press him hard: he may be won...
And he accepts; he enters in:
You'll sup together at the inn.

He takes; he pauses to adore...
Nay, wait! We've seen this done before...
Flash after flash of inward light –
Rabbouni!! – What? No more in sight?

– Of course! We knew it all along!
Those tones to Him alone belong;
That lovely tingling in our hearts
Nought but the Master's grace imparts.

We must go back. We must go back.
The road is long, but these hearts crack
With Joy that will to folly drive –
We've seen Him! Jesus is alive!

(Father Laurence has since set this to music.)

AR ÔL GWELD LLYTHYR MRS JAMES

Mi welais amlen ar y bwrdd o'm blaen –
A mi heb ddisgwyl dim am gyflawn fis.
O'i dal fe wyddwn ddal rhwng ei dwy haen
Ryw bresenoldeb rhwng fy mawd a'm bys.
Myfyriais ar y rhyfedd gyfrin nerth
Sy'n gorffwys yn ddi-stŵr mewn pecyn gwyn;
Ystyriais eto bris dihafal werth
Cain ddefnydd mud yr offerynnau hyn...
Ni fedraf ateb hon nac unrhyw un
A ddaw â darn o'r byd trwy furiau'r gell,
Cans dur ddistawrwydd Rheol lem ei min
A dorrodd atsain ola'r gorwel pell.
Ond ddwywaith yn y flwyddyn cam am awr
Fodloni'r ysfa deimlaf yma 'nawr.

After receiving Easter letters
(and sending a missive that could have important consequences)

An envelope is but a tree grown old,
And chopped and treated till at last 'tis made
A little square, whose emptiness can hold
The fulness of the human heart out-weighed
On sheet on sheet of script inanimate
That nothing knows about the force it holds
Upon the brain that soon shall permeate
The trav'ling Truth this packet now unfolds.
How many hearts have leaped to see this square
Bear their own name, for that they knew within
The presence of the other to be there,
Enclosed, incarnate 'twixt two walls so thin...!
Ignited missile, loaded with my soul,
Explode far, far away, beyond control!

AR ÔL DERBYN LLYTHYR Y TAD LAURENCE

Derbyniais lythyr ddydd neu ddau yn ôl
Ysgytwodd waliau'r unsain, unwedd Gell.
Myfyrdod Hedd a ffôdd ar garlam ffôl
Wrth ganfod gorwel cyfandiroedd pell
Na welai gynt, na wyddai am eu bod
Pan gauodd y Dyfodol ddrws am byth
Ar bob annisgwyl 'fory allai ddod
Â gwên i ddunos y guddiedig nyth.
Fy Nhad yng Nghrist! Ai posib' ydyw hyn,
Y bydd i'r ffurfiau mân a grafaf 'nawr
Ar ddernyn bach di-nod o bapur gwyn,
Wrth siarad wrthyf f'hun o awr i awr,
Ryw ddydd ddymchwelyd muriau carchar du
A chyrraedd llygaid anweledig lu?

1982

After receiving news

And can it be that these soliloquies,
That Thou alone may'st hear, are yet to be
Detected far away beyond the seas
By ears that I know not, that know not me?
O Rule of Silence! thou hast stopped me up;
These ears, this mouth, these fingers thou hast bound.
The Hidden is my portion and my cup;
Thy force doth turn to sin all other sound.
– *I will not sin:* it would defeat the end
Of this strange life, and turn to ridicule
The prayer sent to the One that I offend
E'er adding to this noisy monticule...
Yet, if I stop, th'unsaid rests e'er unsaid,
And what ne'er was ne'er shall be, can be, read.

Le Manuscrit du Purgatoire

The manuscript that lies before my eyes,
Unknown to this wide world – unknown to me
Till yesterday – hath travelled through the skies,
And comes directly, gracious Lord, from Thee.
I hold the greatest gift that I e'er held
(– Save those, e'en greater, common to each soul –):
A joy unknown within my heart hath welled,
My little body bursts my massive cowl:
THIS MUST BE KNOWN! – It is an atom bomb
That Providence hath planted in this cell.
The choice is mine...: It can once more become
Forgotten – as desires the ruse of Hell –
Or, passing through the filter of my brain,
It can, in English, walk the world again.

CYN DECHRAU CYFIEITHU

Llawysgrif fach! A wyddost faint dy werth?
O babur mud! A glywaist d'uchel floedd
A'th effaith arnaf wrth im deimlo nerth
Y gair ddôi mi ddoe o'r Heddiw oedd?
Ie, Heddiw ydoedd hefyd arni hi
A farciai ddoe ar hwn dy femrwn gnawd
Yr hyn ddôi ati o'r Yfory fry
O un a groesodd ffin gwhanfur Rhawd.
Ie, heddiw unais fi â'u Heddiw hwy –
Nid yn y Clas, lle'r oedodd gynt y rhain,
Ond fan lle'r ŷnt, ers canrif bron, ill dwy,
Ddisgrifir arnat gan 'r un aeth o'r blaen
Trwy Uffern puredigaeth dynol-ryw
Am ugain mlynedd, cyn gweld Heddiw Duw.

1982

Yn y gwely

(wythnos y Pasg)

O Gloch ddi-enaid, fythol fyw,
Dy ganiad di yw llais fy Nuw.
Wrth lewni'r dyffryn nos a dydd
A wyddost rym d'awdurdod cudd?

... Y *sine mora* bythol hwn –
"Gad yn y fan a'r lle dy bwn;
Beth bynnag fyddo, ufuddha..."
– Un tinc bob llaw o'i thasg ryddha.

Y lleiaf sain o'th haearn mud
Newidia wedd y Clas i gyd:
Awr ar ôl awr, ddydd ar ôl dydd,
Hyd Angau, trefnu'n rhawd y bydd.

Ac yn y nos fe'n gelwi ni
O ddyfnder cwsg at Engyl fry:
Am deirawr yn y ddunos oer
Noswylio wnawn yng nghwmni'r lloer.

Ond melys ydyw'r gwely gwellt
Yn sŵn y daran hon a'r mellt...
Rhaid dod o hyd i gwsg yn awr –
Fe'm gelwi eto gyda'r wawr.

Y Gyntaf Awr.. y Drydedd Awr...
Y Chweched... Nawfed... seiniant 'nawr.
A'r Gosber gyda hwyr y dydd
At fron fy Iôn yn galw fydd.

O deced ydyw'r alwad hon! –
A'r gyfres ddyletswyddau gron
Yn gyflawn – ond am Weddi'r Nos:
Y Cwmplin – gyda'r *Salve* dlos.

O Wyry addfwyn henffych well!
Mi glywaf, fel pe bai o bell,
Yng nghân y gloch lais Angel Nef
Yn codi megis cyson lef:

"*Ave! Ave!* Mae'r Nef gerllaw:
Bob trawiad, newydd ras a ddaw.
Rho imi glywed *Fiat* gref –
Ymgyfarfyddiad yw â'r Nef."

(Tôn: *Iesu, corona celsior* / *Iam lucis orto sidere*)

EASTER WEEK
(early hours of the morning)

Almighty Bell, voice of my God,
Rule o'er the Cloister by thy nod:
Thou art the king of this small band –
Each sentry waits for thy command

Thy deep, deep voice reverberates.
Thou speakest – every stone vibrates.
The thumping of thy rhythmic strain
Is clapped by every hill and plain.

Each farm, each village heareth thee:
To them thou preachest silently:
They know what this faint echo means,
Each list'ning soul some profit gleans:

"Arise! Prepare to meet your God;
Keep watch! Be girded, vested, shod.
Sev'n times a day lift up your hands –
Lo! calling the muezzin stands."

The eighth is in the heart of night,
In silence deep, 'neath sacred light.
Remember, ye that this sound hear,
That faithful souls keep vigil here.

Good brazen master, sing thy song.
Gargantua, toy with thy gong:
Thy slightest wish is my command –
All little, I before thee stand.

(Melody: *Iam lucis orto sidere*)

Sul y Pasg bach

(cyn gwisgo a dringo at yr Allor)

O gwmwl peraidd, gwmwl mwyn,
Beth ydyw hwn, yr hudol swyn
Sy'n pylu 'meddwl megis gwin
Pan ddêl i'm ffroenau ôl dy rin?

D'aroglau mêl, bereiddiaf darth,
A glywir 'nawr o do hyd barth
Adeilad sanct y Sanct ei hun –
Presennol wyt, Absennol Un.

Addoli wnawn, ymgrymu wnawn:
O sawr y Nef mae'r Tŷ yn llawn.
O thuser, dwg ein gweddi fry,
I lys y Gwynfydedig lu.

Ymgyfarfyddiad yma sydd;
Mae'r Hollol-Arall yma 'nghudd:
Ie, cuddia, cuddia, gyfrin fwg,
A'n traed at ffin Gwaharddiad dwg.

1982

(ar ôl derbyn yr Acolitiaeth a dechrau gwasanaethu fel is-ddiacon yn
yr Offeren Fawr)

(Tôn: *O lux beata*)

PSALM 141, VERSE 2

(Monday after Quasimodo, meditating on new functions as acolyte)

O sacred cloud, sweet mist of prayer,
Up... up... to Heav'n my pleading bear.
With God each stone, each rafter fill,
With mystic trance Man's spirit thrill.

Rise up... rise up..., bear me with thee,
From earth my earth-bound spirit free,
Transport me to that Stygian Shore:
There leave me – dazed, yet craving more.

O! glimpse of far Elysion!
O! distant, faint Trisagion!...
This Odour is not of the earth,
This Ether bathes th'angelic Mirth.

O Thurible, thou burnest me!
O Opium, I ride on thee!
O! Voyage to the great Unknown!
I stand, 'twixt Heav'n and Earth... Alone.

(Melody: *O lux beata*)
Psalm 141: 140 in the Vulgate.

CERDDORIAETH

(Wrth ddychwelyd o'r Plygain, ac ar ôl cyfansoddi'r ail Sanctus)

Fe'th glywais di pan eto'n belen gron
O ddiniweidrwydd dan d'hwi-hwian mwyn...
Yn hŷn fe ddysgais gytgord lleddf a llon
A chyfareddol effaith newydd swyn...
Yn llanc fe ddawnsiais ar d'ysgwyddau di
Am ennyd, nid am hir – nid digon hir
I wybod grym dy grafanc arnom ni
Sy'n teithio orig fach ardd 'Ienctid ir.
... Fe'th glywais heno eto, estron Ffrind,
Yn dod o bell, o bell, o ddyfnder Dyn.
Atseiniodd d'atsain sain y si sy'n mynd
Yn ôl i ddyfnder dyfnder Cân ei hun
Lle clywir *Sanctus* ar ôl *Sanctus* gref
Ar dannau'i sancteiddiolaf donau Ef.

MUSIC
(Immediately after Matins)

A word that means the Muses' own blest art,
Known unto them that coined it, as to those
Who had no words to cover what the heart
Of *homo sapiens* once, once more, knows –
This art he learnt ere e'er he learnt to speak,
– Nay, some would have us say that ere his time,
With unharmonic snout and gentler beak,
His father's father this art used to mime...
O! Beauty's language, I was rocked of thee;
A little older I half-felt thy trance,
And glimpsed what cloisterers shall never see
The hour thou'rt linked to Love's high rhythmic dance...
This night I heard thine echo once again
Rise up and fall and fade on Time's refrain.

CAMERA

Yfory rhewir eiliad fach ddi-nod
Hyd ddiwedd Amser yn dy gylla di.
Mi wn y peidiaf cyn bo hir â bod,
Heb adael cof o'm cyntaf lesni i
Ond am y 'Fory hwn a dry'n hir Ddoe
Ar ddarn o bapur na ŵyr eto ddim
Am lu'r atgofion heddiw mae'n crynhoi –
Ai'n ôl, fel ef, i'r sbwriel, ond am rym
Y dewin hylif a ddarganfu Dyn
Ddwy ganrif 'nôl, trwy waith rhai aeth o'r blaen
I'r ebargofiant gofir gan y llun
Sy'n bloeddio Hanes heb na sŵn na sain.
Yfory rhewir ar goflyfr hwn
A doddo ryw ddydd, hwyrach, ddeigryn crwn.

1982

Carte de Séjour

They tell me that a photograph is due:
Tomorrow I shall see the big wide world
For one short hour, and do what should not do
A good Carthusian who recalls the word
Of Holy Rule that bids ne'er show the face
In portraits, pictures, nor one's name in books.
Obscurity should leave not e'en a trace
On Life's turned page, nor Youth's unused good-looks.
Invention of a century or two!
I know the pow'r of thy strong memory's eye.
Thy captive relived hours have pierced me through
Too often. Nay! thou'rt but a living lie!
My heart, my hands reach out to what they see
Incarnate in unreal eternity.

20/4/82

AFTER RETURNING HOME

I came in contact with a human soul
Across the tent that hid the unknown world
'Neath hs huge wimple, as 'neath my great cowl...
My eyes were closed, when suddenly a word
– The first on uncracked tones to reach mine ear
In six long years – did rouse me from my dreams
To yet another: this, like them, so near
And yet so far, that now once more it seems
More faint, more distant than the furthest one
That ever found its way to this dark cell:
A new-born monk felt burn a new-born nun
And for a second felt within him well
The flood that long ago he too had known,
And saw, as ne'er before, what ne'er was shown.

OCCUPATION: Religieux trappiste

(After coming across the first permis de séjour and recalling what Frère Secrétaire wrote on the form.)

Je pense encore à ce cher monastère
Qui berça ma jeunesse en son doux chant...
La Trappe! – Ah! Qu'est-il? Quel est ce mystère
Qui tire, attire, et puis déchire tant
Le cœur de tout jeune homme qui entend
Ton grand Silence, dont l'aiguë Sirène
Perce à jamais le Plaisir que défend
Ce vaste mur qui rompt la cantilène
De tout ce qui peut tirer sur les cordes
Des cœurs inconnus passés par ici,
Qui portent seuls le monde qui déborde
Cet être jamais fait pour être ainsi?
... Pourtant!... Ce mot *RELIGIEUX TRAPPISTE*
Me parle!!... Aurais-je fait mauvaise piste???

St Vincent Ferrer

Saint Vincent, is it true what these men say,
That thou didst preach in this our noisy town
Here in the pulpit that I touched today
In that blest haven hitherto unknown –
That thou didst preach and preach, and preach again
In gibberish that by some unknown spell
Did myriads for the One thou preachedst gain
And souls snatch from the yawning jaws of Hell?
O crazy Paraclete! Art orthodox?
A market-place was never made for this.
High Latin clarioned from a little box
Could but bring forth a higher boo and hiss.
... Or didst Thou what Thou didst to one loud soul?
– Heat Billy Graham to freeze one mute cowl?

At Prime

Each Thursday I recite a little psalm
That floods my mind with memories of yore.
The sound of this new moon's pure virgin calm
Re-echoes that that reached mine ears before
When on my bended knees at eventide
I joined my voice to that of one fair soul
Who shared my little Psalter at my side
In that small room, that tiny student's hole
That by her presence had become a shrine
Where new-found Grace would work its hounding work
On one small heart that leaned awhile on mine,
Though knowing what barred future did there lurk.
'Tis strange! I that no would-be wife e'er sought
Found many – while such angels Nunhood fought.

BACK TO THE CONVENT
(in thought)

It struck eleven as I said my prayers
In that small convent, on the Public's side
Of that huge grille that sealed my world from theirs –
And both from the great sealed-off world outside.
The office that I prayed was for the dead
Who, 'neath another grille, another world,
Recall these Psalms that they, like us, once said
In unchanged manner, word for unchanged word...
I gazed into the veil that hid my Lord
From me, from these my Sisters, and from them
That wait, like me, like them, the Heav'ns' reward
For those who here themselves to Hell condemn
–When Time struck home what timèd hours did mean.
Two grilles were sawn... I saw 'yond yonder screen.

After receiving Miss W.'s letter

The whole world thinks that we are holy men,
And some would call us *Saints* – not knowing who
Or what hides in this sacred robbers' den
Each day to nail the Crucified anew
By their indifference t'ward the One they touch
Too often – and no more with that *first love*,
– Nay, with entrenched lukewarmness, and that such
As would to tears the hardest human move.
Whip on, Carthusians, fast until your ribs
Rub 'gainst your itching cilice-shirts – and pray
At length within yourselves most fragrant fibs
In well-paid idleness, eight hours a day,
Till Grace, abused, your souls to blazes blast...
While saints that no one hailed be first at last.

Un mot pour toi
(Contrepartie du précédent)

The letter that comes to me on this day
Comes from a living saint – the Real Thing –
Who chose to serve her Lord in every way
Save these, like ours, that bear a holy ring.
I learnt from this pure soul what prayer did mean
Not through her treatise on the four degrees,
Nor by her beads by all the parish seen –
For rarely did I catch her on her knees –
But – Lord, forgive me! – by the way she smelt,
For she did breathe Thee in and breathe Thee out,
And when I hugged her 'twas Thy hug I felt
In aged Virginity that Youth did flout...
And since enclosed, each morn at 8 a.m.
My prayer joins hers through whose I'm where I am.

PARDON ME...

Saint Vincent, I come back to thee again
– E'en though thou'rt dead and gone six hundred years.
Tell me one thing: These souls that thou didst gain,
These hardened sinners melted into tears,
This Pow'r thou hadst, – was this, were these, thine own,
Or did another work for thee, in thee?
"Thou needest not the answer. 'Tis well-known:
The words th'Apostle said, he said for me."
Nay, that I know, good Saint; it was thy Lord.
Yet why for thee? Why this abundant fruit?
And this small pulpit whence came forth thy word,
Is't in a place that doth its history suit?
Think hard! Think hard, good Saint: was't p'haps not these
Who moved the world, unmoved on their sore knees?

TROIS HEURES DU MATIN, UN VENDREDI

«Mais ça fait mal!» dit le novice à son saint Maître.
– C'est fait pour ça», fit celui-ci, en souriant.
– Pas sérieux, dit à son tour le nouveau prêtre,
Austérité bien sucrée pour les friands!
Ce n'est pas ça qui réduira mon Purgatoire:
Ce qui me coûte, c'est le pain qui va avec!»
... C'est vrai, c'est vrai on cherche trop sa propre gloire.
La Sainteté réside-t-elle en ce pain sec?
Ce petit fléau qui fera un peu de bruit
Pendant quelques minutes, est-il si méchant?
... Et pourtant!... – Quand je songe, ô Monde, que, la nuit,
Ces membres nus frappés sont, chez toi, alléchants,
Je me demande si en fait je frappe en vain.
Qu'il vienne ici, qui ronfle et dort avec dédain!

(The bread was nice and soft today. That's why the knife gave in first.)

After receiving Blake's poem
(My Mother bore me in the Southern wild...)

I often wonder what I really am –
An Englishman baked in an Oxbridge school,
Ai Cymro pybyr, mab i bybyr fam
A brawd i frawd a gân i Saeslyd ffŵl,
Ou même si je ne suis devenu
Tout autre chose par ce long exil
Si différent de tout ce qu'a connu
Un Gallois, pourtant bien anglophile...
An neutrum quid sim, sicut omnes qui
Sub hoc cucullo antiquo cantant quæ
Antiqui sempre solitarii
Cantabant ubi et ego hodie.
῝Η εἰμι ὥσπερ σύ, ὦ Κύριε –
Μελχισέδεκ τις, ὤν μέν, ἄπων δέ;

Ai Cymro...: "Or a staunch Welshman, son of a staunch mother
And brother to a brother who sings to a Sasonach-loving fool?

῝Η εἰμι....: "Or am I as Thou art Thyself, Lord –
Perhaps some Melchisedek, having being, yet not being here?"

DIWEDD EBRILL

Mi glywaf sain na chlywais gynt
Yn araf dreiddio tonnau'r gwynt...
Gyfarwydd, anghyfarwydd sain!
Nid ydwyt heddiw fel o'r blaen.

Beth ydyw'r cyfareddol swyn
A deimlaf heno'n d'alwad fwyn?
A ddichon llais aderyn mân
Droi calon brudd yn drystiog gân?

O angel haf! A ddaethost ti
I oerfel maith f'unigedd i?
A ddywaid llef dy neges bell
Fod hoe i benyd creulon gell?

Do, daeth yr awr i lawnehau:
Mae'r Fendith yma i'w mwynhau.
Yn araf, tawdd pelydrau'i Haul
Hir ryndod corff ac enaid gwael.

Dihuna, Natur! Cwyd o'th fedd!
Dewch, greaduriaid oll, i'r wledd!
Ie, brwysgwch dan rasusau'ch Duw!
Chwi reddfau Bywyd, dewch yn fyw...

Yr Atgyfodiad Cosmig sydd
Yn chwyddo holl wythiennau'r pridd.
Pob had, pob croth gynhyrfa'n awr
Dan ledrith y llesmeiriol Sawr.

O henffych well, gyfarwydd sain!
Fe'th glywais, do, fil gwaith o'r blaen:
Ond heddiw holltaist ti fy mron:
Cân, Gwcw, d'Aleliwia lon!

(Tôn: *Ad cænam Agni*, sef tôn Gosber y Pasg)

Lettre incandescente
(Auditu auris audivi de te, nunc autem oculus meus videt te.*)

Encore un billet de cet Au-delà
Que trop de monde taxe d'être obscur;
Encore une âme envoyée ici-bas,
Séparée toutefois par ce grand Mur
Qu'elle aurait bien voulu pouvoir rompre
Une heure, un instant – juste assez pour faire
Cet acte qui eût seul pu interrompre
Au bout d'un siècle ou deux la grande affaire...
«Arrête!» dit cette ombre à la croyante
Qui priait pour la paix d'un esprit cher –
Et qui, hélas, devint la clairvoyante
Qui dut écrire un billet pour l'enfer.
Oui, Oui! Son âme-sœur a dit ceci:
«Écris... pour que nul autre n'entre ici!»

*Job 42:5

END OF APRIL

Mine ears perceive a distant sound,
My pen a theme for song hath found,
My lips, my heart, too long unused,
Have sensed a Joy to sense refused

I walk alone in this small cell,
In silence wait the Vesper bell –
And lo! I hear a fairer call,
So clear, so near, yet e'er so small.

The Easter Song is pealing out,
With tiny lung my friend doth shout:
He hails me, hails thee, hails the world –
Th'Arisen's banners are unfurled!

Rise, resurrect! all Nature's powers;
The Victory is yours, is ours:
The Lord of Life is passing through
Creation's slowly changing hue.

Each seed, each womb, burst! Open up!
Drink deeply from this mystic Cup
Of dream-producing Nectar pure –
Yield gently: 'tis a Godhead's lure!

Vibrate, rotate 'neath Earth's high trance –
The Universe herself doth dance.
The Risen One is raising us:
Thou hadst, gay Cuckoo, to sing thus.

(Melody: *Ad cænam Agni providi*)

NOSON GLIR
(ar ôl y Plygain)

Yn oriau bach y bore mwyn,
Wrth glywed y plygeiniol swyn,
Edrychaf drwy ffenestri 'medd,
Wen Seren Fore, ar dy wedd.

'Rwyt yno'n llosgi'n henaidd dân
Nos ar ôl nos, â'th olau glân
Yn cadw golwg arnom ni
Tra canwn glod dy Grëwr di.

Cyhoeddi'r wyt, fel ni, i'r byd
Sy'n gorwedd 'nawr mewn trymgwsg clyd
Fod newydd ras gerllaw i ddyn
Pan ddeffry o'i anghofus hun.

Mae cyfle newydd, newydd wawr,
Mae diwrnod arall, arall awr
Yn dechrau – gyda'i drysor oll
O ras am ras aeth gynt yngholl.

O ddyn! Pe gwypit werth un dydd! –
Cyn hir dy nos heb wawriad fydd,
Heb seren dlos i'th wahodd fry
At ras di-drai'n Cynhaliwr cu.

Bydd diwedd i'r goleuni mwyn,
Bydd melltith lle bu unwaith swyn;
Camddefnydd gras a dry yn sur –
Budreddi! – lle bu crisial pur.

Na, heddiw, heddiw cwyd o'th win;
Yf ddawn y Nef, a theimla rin
A gwawl Paradwys pur dy Iôr –
Yf! Llynca, bodda'n nafn o'i fôr.

(Tôn: *Æterne rerum Conditor* / *Splendor paternæ gloriæ*, sef emynau'r
nos: Plygain / Moliannau)

A CLEAR NIGHT
(After matins)

When I behold thee, Morning Star,
And see thee coming from afar,
I look and look, and look again
Beyond the realm of Time's domain.

Thou comest hither as of yore,
Thou dost as thou hast done before
Morn after morn, since that first Morn
When morning Light herself was born.

Thou art the newness ever new
That ancient Adam also knew:
Fair Matutina, burning still,
Forerunning Dawn o'er wave and hill.

Cast out thy silver rays of hope
T'ward Earth that after thee doth grope;
In silence deep proclaim the word
Of Glory to a darkened world

Soft boreal Light, thy life is short:
Thine own eclipse thou dost escort.
Efface thyself before thy lord,
Recede... recede... without a word.

And when this day is fully spent,
And man hath used what God hath lent,
Shine forth again, 'neath altered name –
Sweet Vespera, e'er, e'er the same.

(Melody: *Æterne rerum Conditor/Splendor paternæ gloriæ*)

Wrth fynd yn ôl i gysgu

Wrth dawel gau f'amrannau'n hyfryd swyn
Dyfnderoedd Nos, er d'weddi hyn o hun
A ganiateir gan drefn Rhagluniaeth fwyn
I hyd yn oed ein Rheol lem ei min,
Meddyliaf, "Tybed pa ryfeddod ffraeth,
Pa wlad anhygoel sydd ar ffin nesáu
I'm twyllo eto â'i hafreal Ffaith,
I'm hadfodloni yn fy ffug fwynhau?"
...Bu imi lawer gwaith ailganfod rhai
A gerais gynt, a gweled eto'r dref
A'm carodd i – ond fel pe'n mynd yn llai
Nes toddi 'mhell mewn rhyw ellyllaidd nef...
O rithiau mwyn, sy'n dal i ddod yn ôl,
A ŵyr a'ch piau am eich crwydro ffôl?

1982

After Night Office

The voice of Prayer is ever heard on high:
I sleep, but others keep the lamp alive.
My resting lungs now heave a little sigh
As slowly it strikes on from four to five –
As they recall how each unthinking beat
Calls forth the brethren to those stalls that knew
A gyrovague who in his youthful heat
From cloister unto cloister madly flew –
And fell in love too often with that Love
That did without a word reverberate
In those arched tunnels through which e'en now move
Those hooded mysteries that contemplate.
La Trappe! I fell too early in thy jaws.
The hiraeth for my home mine inwards gnaws.

The First of May

Shall I forget the word that once was said
By that small harbour, those small bobbing boats,
As three young souls, each pledged to rest unwed,
Exchanged their views in serious, solemn notes –
When summer Warmth had thawed the ice within
And lightened, shortened what enticed without,
When in the air rang sweet, magnetic Sin,
And God's own gifts made God's strange robbing doubt –
The word one head that now 'neath wimples lies
Could no more hold within its unused breast,
When suddenly it looked into the eyes
Of one that walked the rope of that same test:
"...But when it comes, it's hard; it's very hard.
SPRING FEVER! Yet it's sometimes very hard." ?

LLYTHYR

Dywedir wrthyf fod rhyw waith ar waith
Yng Ngwalia acw – er na chlywaf ddim
I'w brofi yma ond distawrwydd maith
Hir aros am newyddion gwyllt eu grym
Ar glustiau meudwy glyw ond 'chydig iawn
O newydd bethau 'ngofod byd di-stŵr?
Beiriannau Dyn! Dofasoch egni Duw!
Fe'ch crewyd, fel eich crëwr, yn ddi-sain,
Ond cofiwch ei bob gair heb glust na chlyw –
A'i sgrechain dros y byd â llais mor fain
Na chlywo, welo neb eich tonnau'n dod
Â churiad calon meudwy mud trwy'r rhod.

1982

Beiriannau Dyn...: Recordiwyd ein sgyrsio, ac 'roedd sôn am ddefnyddio'r cynnwys.

DREAMS

When I am wrenched from Hypnos' gentle arms –
In time to wrench my brethren in their turn –
I leave behind a world of Eastern charms
And in a second all I learnt unlearn.
O Wonderland! Had I but at my side
When lost in thee, one tiny writing pad,
The gates of this strange heav'n I'd open wide
And freeze for e'er the frizzling joys I had.
It is bizarre! How rarely doth my soul
Walk proudly through thine absent alley-ways
Clad, as it should be, in the sacred cowl
That should preserve it in this naughty maze!
Dark Land! Did men know what monks did in thee,
They'd flee till death the Saints' bad company.

APRÈS UN SONGE

Et pourtant, est-ce vrai qu'il est ainsi –
Qu'en rêve on cesse d'être ce qu'on est,
Que ceux qui passent par ce pays-ci
Font tout, mais tout – oui, tout – comme il leur plaît?
Que c'est bizarre! Je n'y comprends rien!
Très rarement habillé comme il faut,
Mais retenu toujours par quelque Lien,
Marqué jusqu'au dedans par quelque Sceau,
Mon être réagit inconsciemment
En ce qu'il ne peut jamais cesser d'être:
Une âme qui raisonne sciemment,
Qui sent ce que ressent son très-saint Maître.
Chartreux je suis, chartreux je reste en rêve,
Sauf qu'un de mes habits fut fait par Ève.

JUST ANOTHER DAY

Matins are sung, and sleep returns
To heavy eyelids that have kept
Prayer's silent Lamp, that onward burns,
Vigilant o'er the Prayer that slept.

Now as I dose I hear the sound
That, far away, doth others rouse.
For them e'en now begins the Round
Of sacred duties in thy house.

Onward and onward as I sleep
The Torch is passed from quire to quire:
Convent on convent now doth keep
Each in its turn the Vestal fire.

Through the night Calm I hear as 'twere
Faint, distant echoes of that chant
That e'en the hardened heart doth stir,
That makes the Spirit Godward pant.

(*Excitatio*)

Now, even now, 'tween three and four,
Trappists file in without a word,
Watching while men in comfort snore,
Singing to Earth's forgotten Lord.

On hill, in vale, as beacons bright,
Quire after quire strikes up anew,
Hallowing th'air of sinful Night,
Paying the Holy homage due.
    (*the Holy: le Saint*)

Sleep will have gained mine eyes again
Ere Bennet's sons take up the Light.
Onward I'll sleep as Prayer's sweet strain
From Carmel's peace pervades the night.

... And so it was: sleep took my soul!
Now 'tis my turn to join my voice
– When I have found my frock, my cowl –
To this vast Hymn, with lesser noise.

For 'tis in silence that I sing:
Only my breath doth cross my lips;
Yet, as I hear this Prime bell ring,
My prayer into a greater slips:

One in my quire, I'm one with all
Who at this hour these psalms recite:
From sea to sea, in pew and stall,
Monks, sisters, faithful now unite...

And greet with me the Sabbath dawn,
Offer with me its first-fruits sweet
Deep in the calm of waking Morn,
Laid – ere't be soiled – before thy feet.

(*Thanksgiving*)

Time hath moved on and Terce hath rung,
Ending our meditations deep,
High Mass, 'mid incense sweet, is sung,
And once again our cells we keep.

(*Midday*)

Time is so short, O Lord, so short!
Now as I write Sext too is passed.
The fast is broken, now in thought
O'er this brief day mine eyes I cast.

None, from which Noon doth draw its name,
– E'en though 't be later than its time –
Calls us again to tend Prayer's Flame:
Halted I'll be by its first chime

And so it is! – The warning bell
Rings as I trace one last wee line...
O! noisy solitary bell!
How for the peaceful World I pine!

(*Before Vespers*)

> And None was sung... and Faults were said,
> As we before the altar lay,
> Prostrate before our earthly head,
> Whipped for the frailty of our clay.

(*Evening*)

> Now I await the Vesper call –
> *Vêpres!* – blest prayer of Mother Church,
> Sung in each convent, great and small,
> Dear to all souls that solace search.

> ... And song was heard... and sins were washed
> In Absolution's sacred stream...
> Now to all noise the door I've latched,
> And once again I lonely seem.

(*Lectio Divina*)

> Yet is it so, good Lord? Sweet Lord,
> Is't not of all the sweetest hour?
> *Reading Divine* – O Sacred Word!
> Here in Night's peace make heard thy power.

(*Recollectio*)

      Let me in this last precious prayer
      Leave far behind the noise of words.
      Let me but know that Thou art there:
      L'examen breath for thought affords.

      Lord, I think on... and on... and on.
      This day is passed – as 'twere unfelt;
      Each prayer is said, each duty done:
      Once more I kneel where first I knelt.

(*Compline*)

      Each day will pass as this one, God!
      Compline to Compline counts the beat
      Of Life's accelerating plod,
      Time's rhythmic fierce goose-stepping feet

      Soon will the bell close off the day:
      Th'Angelus and *le Grand Silence*
      Will seal in peace its hours for aye
      – And these mine eyes in somnolence.

      ... And so it was.

                             (On rhythm of melody composed for it)

CES PAGES JAUNISSANTES...

On t'appelle la Sœur qui s'appelle Sans-nom,
L'Anonyme qui mourut sans bruit, sans renom,
Un beau jour vers la fin de ce siècle de foi
En la vraie Incroyance appuyée sur les lois
De la Raison.
       Ô! Sœur oubliée de ce monde,
Enterrée sous la boue d'une haine profonde
Par ces grands raisonneurs qui entendent refaire
Les décrets éternels régissant d'autres aires,
Avec tout ce qui plane en ce Vide si plein
De surprises, fournies par ce Dieu en déclin,
Que ton âme, ma Sœur, a trouvé vigoureux
Dans un ciel réformé un peu plus rigoureux
Qu'une sœur – même bonne – ne l'eût jamais pensé –
Surtout si celle-ci avait trop offensé
Cette Fable innocente, incapable de nuire
À une âme qui sait en ce monde la fuir.

Oui, ma Sœur, j'ai eu peur en relisant ta lettre –
Lettre? Non! – très précieuse – oui, unique – fenetre
Sur ce monde inconnu que connaît maintenant
Et ton âme et la mienne, car ce Continent
Qu'on reproche de rester voilé à nos yeux
Se devoile en ses traits les plus nus et hideux
À travers ces messages, ces cris si étranges
Reçus jour après jour et transmis par cet ange
Inconnu comme toi, comme toi effacé,

Dont la plume sans voix fait hurler le passé
Pour les siècles des siecles, et – chose encor pire –
Fait résonner les sons de ce monde à venir
Qui est déjà venu, qui ne partira pas –
Cauchemar éternel qui un jour se montra
Un peu plus sérieux que ne l'auraient voulu
Ces très grands connaisseurs d'un plus grand Inconnu.
Vingt années de souffrance! – et cela bien moins
Que le taux général qu'en ce pays lointain
Les nouveaux-arrivés trouvent sur leur bilan
Le matin où se trouve au delà de l'Écran –
Sans le vouloir, d'ailleurs – tout leur être – et cette âme
Qui a trop souvent bu à ce ruisseau infâme
Que les savants dénomment – sans toujours le fuir
(Sachant où son absence pourrait les conduire)
–COMPROMIS.

    Ô! gros Monstre cornu, plein d'astuce!
– Qui se plante en nos cœurs comme l'œuf d'une puce
Et qui pousse et qui pousse en beau gras parasite,
Puis arrange à ses goûts et le lieu et le site
De son action –
    Oui, toi! C'est à toi que je pense,
Petit *oui* du début par lequel tout commence.
Pour reculer ici il suffit d'arrêter
– Même pas! – C'est assez de ne plus avancer...

Allons donc! A-t-on vraiment à être si dur?
Une entorse ici... là... ne te rend pas impur –

Et c'est fait! On a cessé de viser le but,
Et perdu pour toujours cet *amour du début*
Qui eût su nous conduire à ce Seul Nécessaire –
Devenu maintenant tout à fait secondaire –
Par un *oui*, juste un *oui*, jamais vu ni senti,
Qui va faire qu'un saint n'aura pas abouti
À ce degré de gloire préparé pour lui –
Bien plus, qu'il va vivre sans zèle et sans fruit
Comme toi.

   Ô ma Sœur! Ô ma Sœur! Que c'est triste!

Oui,
   SUNT LACRYMÆ RERUM!
       Quelle affreuse piste!
Qui t'a conduit, me conduit, qui conduit le monde
À ce lieu de supplice où tes larmes profondes
Ont jailli, puis coulé lentement jusqu'à nous,
Transformées en cette encre qui nous dépeint tout
Ce que tu as trouvé derrière le Voile,
Et pourquoi tu as pleuré la nuit sans étoiles
De l'Aurore.
    Ta gloire était grande en nos bouches:
Tu es morte victime d'un acte qui touche
Même un cœur endurci à la grâce de Dieu –
On t'a crue toute prête pour l'entrée aux cieux
Qui t'attendaient.
     Mais non!
       Tu attendais toujours
Quand ta voix sans larynx cria grâce un beau jour:

«Aidez-moi! Aidez-moi à sortir de ce lieu,
Car mon âme est parmi les plus grands miséreux!»

Chère sœur, sœur aînee! Tu m'apprends où je vais:
Car l'état de mon âme, Dieu seul le connaît –
Mais je sais tout au moins que si tu nous dis vrai,
Le Plaisir que j'ai eu, je l'ai eu à mes frais.

RUMINATING FATHER LAURENCE'S LETTER

My brother held one morning in his hand
A little tin but half an inch in height.
He placed within its gizzard one small band
And left it in a corner out of sight...
And chattered on as though nought were amiss,
As brother talks with brother when alone
'Twixt four thick walls, in silence such as this,
An hour or two, like any, quickly flown.
The words we spoke tipped slowly to the past
Like those of any day, that no more thought
Recalls – for seldom doth our mind e'er cast
A second glance o'er what returns to nought;
– And yet, it seems that what we said that day,
Through that small list'ning tin, was said for aye.

Il y a deux courants dans l'Ordre...

The words we utter are, as these men say,
As dead as dead can be... and killing me.
In repetition vain we homage pay
To one who talked of prayer in Verity.
The cows of Bashan and the likes of Og
Move to and fro 'mid strange desilvered wings.
In swinging 'Eighty-two we're still agog
At how much gore can ooze from naughty kings.
... And yet!... When I reflect how words so dead
Were writ, translated, copied, handed on,
How many meditations they have fed,
How these small blobs this night do what they've done
Since Charlemagne – nay, since the early Church –
'Tis hard to leave this nonsense in the lurch.

As dead...: "Latin is a dead, dead language,
As dead as dead can be.
It killed the ancient Romans,
And now it's killing me."

Connais-tu l'épître de Saint-Jacques?

The Silence of the cell hath taught me, Lord,
The pow'r of this wee thing we call the Tongue.
For those who enter here, the spoken word
Is banished – for it doth to Thee belong.
But I recall how when 'twas yet unbound
This instrument knew little of the Force
In each inanimate yet living sound
It made from nought in teeming intercourse.
I had a friend, through whom I learnt what meant
The meeting of two souls entwined by Talk:
For when at length our words were wholly spent,
We talked no more, but did in silence walk.
... And I perceived, as she talked on in song,
That Contact starts where stops the nervous Tongue.

Y PEDWERYDD O FAI

O! ryfedd weledigaeth ydyw hon
– Gyrhaeddodd fel trwy hap fy nwylo i –
Roed gynt i'r nid anenwog *Fynach Llon*
Cyn ffoi ohono d'erch gynteddau Di.
'Sgrifenna – er ei warth – pa fodd y bu
I'w hyfdra lwyddo tynnu gair o'r brawd
Oedd ar fin troi yn ôl i'w Famwlad gu –
Addewid, medd, y soniai am ei ffawd...
Anghofiwyd am y cwbl oll, medd ef.
Ond un liw nos, pan wnai a wnaf yn awr,
Daeth neges 'nôl o entrych ucha'r nef –
Adroddiad am a welwyd gyda'r Wawr;
– A gair o rybudd o'r tu draw i'r Llen:
Nad ffordd y Brenin ydoedd ffordd y nen.

1982

Ond un liw nos, pan wnai a wnaf yn awr: myfyrdod yr hwyr.

Ysywaeth! Ni wrandawodd ar y rhybudd, ac am i'w fywyd lliw-gar dros Ewrob wedyn ennill enw iddo iddo'i hun y cyfeirir ato fel y Mynach Llon. Cromwell ei hun a drosglwyddodd y llawysgrif, ym-hlith holl ddogfennau'r achos, i swyddogion Harri'r Wythfed. Gel-lir ei darllen heddiw yn y Llyfrgell Brydeinig. (Yr un Mynach Llon ddywedodd, wrth agor ei droell fwyd un diwrnod, "Ah! J'aimerais mieux manger un crapaud que ce poisson-là!" Atebwyd ei gais gan Ragluniaeth. Am fis cyfan ni welwyd ond llyffantod duon yn ei gell, er gwaetha'i holl ymdrechion i'w llosgi. Yn wir, daeth aroglau an-nioddefol o'i ffwrn drwy gydol y mis.)

Lest we forget
(written on the fourth of May)

Had I been born beneath another star
A few more moons ago – yet still had heard
The Calling of my Master from afar,
And let my feet to walls like these be stirred,
I'd not – as I am now – be nibbling bread,
Or brooding o'er who might have been a wife,
But offering a slip-knot my starved head
And waiting for the kind castrator's knife.
O England! On this day thy pastures green
First drank the blood of those, like me, who loved
The Sacrifice that all thy kings had seen,
Ere for one's night of bliss 'twas e'er removed.
... And yet, need I have been so stubborn too?
The priests he made can do just as we do.

The priests he made...: Written while meditating on Leo XIII's
Apostolicæ Curæ.

Same day

PÆTE, NON DOLET! – O bold intrepidity!
Glory of all Womankind's masculinity!
Yet, Arria, didst thou tell us the verity?
Doth agony not hurt at all?

What feels the soul when the body is suffering
Things that the mind cannot learn without shuddering?
Can it be so, that some saints without whimpering
 Bore to the end th'unbearable?

... This is the day on which England's own treachery
Turned on its traitors with Satan's own savagery:
Now, at this hour, unto well-refined butchery
Through London's streets our Fathers trailed.

Tell me, my Brethren, what things did your spirit feel
When the first touch of the carver's well-sharpened steel
Made all your being 'neath hell's own contortions reel
Till hell no more could hold its pain?

And now 'tis o'er, tell me, which is your preference?
Could you once more live the hour of your going hence,
Could you yourself write the blue-print of Providence,
What is the Fate ye'd weave yourself?

Th'answer, my friend, thine own brother hath given thee
When on that night from the depths of Eternity
He cried, "Alas! Alas! Thrice blessèd butchery!
Ne'er for all time shall I hold the palm!"

(Melody: *Sanctorum meritis inclyta gaudia*)

Arria...: The elder Arria, who, during the Stoic resistance to the Emperor, thrust the dagger into her own breast before handing it to her husband Paetus, with the above words.

Th'answer...: A lay-brother who had died before the persecution had appeared to one young choir-monk who was later to yield to the King's wishes, and had warned him beforehand.

Wrth gwrs cei di weld Glyn y Groes

Wrt feddwl am y Wlad a'm magodd i
A'r traed sancteiddiodd gynt eu herwau mwyn...
Wrth blygu unwaith eto i'th Wyddfod Di
A chlywed fel o'r blaen ei Chwa'n fy nwyn
'Nôl... 'nôl... i'w plith, fel rhyw gyfarwydd Wynt,
Daw hiraeth am y dyddiau nad ŷnt mwy
I'w gweled, clywed lle y clywid gynt
O glas i glas, o blwy' i glasaidd blwy',
A glywaf wrth dy Allor heno, Iôr,
Yn sain y ddigyfnewid, fythol Siant
A ddringai'n Echdoe 'Nglwlad o'r cyfryw gôr
O ddyfnder calon gudd mil ddirgel sant
A deimlodd ddoe a deimlaf yma 'nawr
Dan debyg Allor,yn nharth tebyg sawr.

1982

Chapître des coulpes

Fe'm chwipiwyd fwy nag unwaith am y Bai
Beiusaf un dan reol mynaich mud.
Yr ysfa gyfathrachu hon a wnâi
I'r Aelod caeth rith-ffoi'i ddigyfaill fyd.
Langue yw ei enw yn ei fyd ei hun
(Cans enwyd ef ar ôl yr hyn a'i wnaeth) –
O'r offerynnau oll y lleiaf un,
Ond awdur holl lyfryddiaeth Ffug a Ffaith...
O goblin bach! Cêst ryddid ennyd awr,
Ond buost fyw heb wybod am dy fod.
Ymorfffwys yn dy ymddeoliaeth 'nawr,
Ac edrych 'nôl dros d'einioes wag, ddi-nod.
Brad! Brad! Pe gwelswn gynt egnïon hwn...
Ah! Douce Trappe!... Mw wn. *Rhy hwyr!* Mi wn...

1982

Yn Ôl i Lyn y Groes

"Beth ydy' pwrpas mynach," meddai hi,
A minnau'n eistedd ar silff ffenest' fu,
– Heb weld i mewn i'r boenus eironi
'Nghudd yn ymholiad byr ei mynwes gu.
"Fe eilw'r Arglwydd rai...," awn yn fy mlaen,
– Heb ddangos rhith na rhych o'r rhyfedd straen
A gadwyd yn rhy hir dan estron glo.
Cans gwyddwn fod fy ngheiriau'n dod yn ôl
O'r muriau oedd o'n cylch – o'r cwmwl cudd
Adawodd ar y cerrig mud ei ôl –
I un a guddiai ddeigryn ar ei rudd
Wrth wybod fod dwy alwad yn y fan,
Fod gwaliau chwâl yr afdail eto i lan.

1982

Y DDIHANGFA

Mi dreuliais gryn dri mis heb yngan gair
Ond wrthyt Ti – er clywed mwy nag un,
A'u clywed ddwywaith cystal yn yr aer
Wacawyd o sain gorlawn gwacter Dyn...
Gwnâi, brifai ar y dechrau; yna daeth
Yr annolmalrwydd yn normalrwydd byw.
Yr hyn oedd 'nôl, 'mhell... bellach 'nôl yr aeth,
A daeth fy nwifr o hyd i donfedd Duw,
Na chipiwyd gynt, gan drwch y gofod praff
O'm blaen, o'm hôl – mwy fyth, o'm mewn fy hun.
Diddymdra wnaeth glust f'enaid yn fwy craff,
I glywed Dyn, byd Dyn, byd calon Dyn.
... A sylwedolais, wrth ddod 'nôl i'm bedd,
Mai sain Marwolaeth ydoedd mamiaith Hedd.

1982

AFTER WAKING UP AN HOUR TOO SOON

It would be so much nicer to sleep on
And on... and on... than, watching, to repress
Those stifled yawns that every moine and nonne
In France at this weird hour heaves ne'ertheless.
The Rule Says, *Yawn ye not,* – yet yawn I will –
Not of mine own accord, but as yawned on
By Brother Ass, who'll bray his plaint until
He gets the little bit that was forgone.
... And yet, who'll know what things a soul doth miss
When 'neath the fastened world of unope'd eyes?
Had I slept on I'd ne'er have written this –
One hour redeemed one ageless word now buys.
... And I, like this, could also not have been,
Had one small hour ticked on 'neath Sleep's blind screen.

FATHER PRIOR IS BECOMING MORE AND MORE DEAF

I rubbed my ear to take away the wax
That blocked the soul within from th'outside world...
And I reflected how our good Prior lacks
The means by which to touch the living word.
Alas! Alas! for those who no more can
Keep silence, and receive as well as give.
Those hidden things hid by the heart of Man
Are known to those alone who've learnt to live
With th'Art of List'ning – Lord! the art that Thou
In thine eternal Silence hast us taught:
For speaking not, but list'ning, Thou dost know
The very Thought that thinks
'neath th'unthought thought...
... And is't for this state that Adam henceforth wears
One sole, closed, mouth, but two wide open ears?

Are you there, Lord?

'Tis strange! E'en when we're utterly alone
Th'unuttered word can speak so loudly that
The workings of the heart be full o'erthrown
As though we with a living being sat.
This night I did but glimpse a passing word
When from the blue two tears came trickling down.
I read of one who saw a darkened world,
But had a way of seeing of his own.
John Paul! – whom we Christ visible do call –
This little child desired so much – like me –
To see the Face behind closed sight's sealed wall
That he cried out, *Come closer, let me see!*
– And so he did, with fingers that perceived
The Presence in which blind faith had believed.

Cofiwch werthfawrogi'ch braint

Soniasoch, Mam, am *ffenest' enaid Dyn*
Wrth ganu marwnadau gwydrau'r *Tab.*
A sylweddolech bwysau geiriau sy'n
Hir dreiddio ystyr *ffenest'* i gaeth fab?
Vilescunt assueta, meddwn i
Y bore'r aethoch ymaith at eich taith
O'n digyfnewid lom olygfa ni
At fil amryliw luniaidd randir fraith.
Eich llygaid ysent am weld rhywbeth gwell
Na'r un o'r blaen – a hwnnw'n well na'r cynt –
Ac er ei weld rhaid ydoedd mynd ymhell,
Heb golli awr, ar frys, ar ffynig hynt...
Gan adael un am flwyddyn yn ei gell
Ddi-symud, â Golygfa dipyn gwell.

1982

You have problems of Turvey dimensions

I had a friend who lived behind a screen
That was e'en denser than the one I know.
His friendship taught me what the Dark doth mean,
And I glimpsed then what I see clearly now.
For I perceived that he perceived far more
Than I with my two eyes that looked at all
They met – for, seeing e'er his inmost core,
His spirit never walked beyond Thought's wall.
He told me what one sees when one sees not,
How lamp-posts can be heard when far too close,
How little things were rarely e'er forgot,
How he beheld a person through his nose...
... And now I understand; for I too see
 Things I ne'er saw ere shown Obscurity.

YN YSTOD MIS YR ADOLYGU
(at yr arholiad)

O dirion Gell! Fe'm cedwi yn dy fynwes
Rhag ofer eriau Dyn a dwndwr Byd.
Mewn oeraidd oes fe'th gaed yn aelwyd gynnes,
I unig feudwy ti wyt annedd glyd.

Cymar fy enaid ydyw tudalennau
Cyfrol ar gyfrol o ysgrifau'r saint.
Cewri ein Doe'r llythrennau hyn ddarllenai,
Ymborth i'w hympryd hwythau yma gaent.

Tad ar ôl Tad eisteddai 'ngolau'r gannwyll
Oes ar ôl oes yng nghwmni'r muriau hyn:
'Run ydyw sain unigedd noson dywyll,
Ac atsain bell y gloch yn teithio'r glyn.

Nid ydyw Amser heddiw'n troi'n wahanol
I'r hyn a wnâi i'r rhai oedd yma gynt:
Llanc... 'ffeiriad... abad...gerddodd i'r Gorffennol –
Gam ar ôl cam, dilynaf innau'u hynt.

Tua'r Goleuni aethant, af, awn ninnau,
Ochr wrth ochr, cell yn erbyn cell.
Ie, 'r un Gras sy'n disgyn arnaf innau
Â'r afon gref a'u dug at Wlad sydd well.

(Tôn: *Rhys*, 433)

Lines ruminated in the Necessarium

A rumour roams that War is simmering
Down in the deep blue sea of Arctica –
Or was it the Antarctic's chilly ring?
– None knows; or if he does, ne'er says Boo-Bah.
It is just as it was some years ago
When engines of destruction flew all 'round,
But where they went none here did ever know,
For through these walls ne'er seeped one earthly sound.
– I tell a lie! The news did enter in,
And that in quantity, from day to day:
Each monk could read at length of Hitler's din,
For at each noon the world press came his way.
And yet for six long years none e'er aught knew,
For Prior said, 'Twas only for the 1—.

"How good of God to make your nose stop... here,"
He mused (– perhaps comparing mine with his,
– Or hers whose curve did this world's hist'ry steer),
While I, perplexed, thought, "How odd Father is!"
Wee nose! Thou'rt often blocked – nay, so much so
That surgeons have once rummaged in thy bowels –
Yet 'tis through thee that these mine inwards know
The emanations that can stir our souls.
For since the day when thou no more didst find
Aught else to sniff save him on whom thou'rt fixed,
Thy doubly sharpened edge his blunted mind
Hath sawn asunder more than once betwixt
What it breathes in from day to endless day
And thine electric shocks from Yesterday.

Cher Docteur A...

Le Père Prieur ne désire pas que je sorte de nouveau. Mais j'ai bien plaisir de vous informer que le changement de paillasse a eté très efficace. Votre nasalissime client...

Or hers...: Cleopoatra's, of whose nose it was said that had it been a fraction longer, the course of world history might have been different.

Resurgam

Ô Sélignac! Quand je t'ai vue ce soir
Si triste et si délaissée – arrivée
Au bout de tes vieux jours – j'ai cru revoir
Les traits de l'avenir en ton passé.
Condamné à la mort, ton cœur raidi
Ne savait plus les airs de sa jeunesse
Appris en ce pays de mélodies
Où vit le jour ta vieille, vieille messe.
Tes murs sans voix, témoins de l'Inconnu
Que seuls connaissent ceux que connaît Dieu,
Se souvenaient de ceux qu'ils avaient vu
Aller à Lui en passant par ce lieu.
Tu vis encor, ma Mère – et m'as conçu
En ton vieux sein...
            – Mais, demain, vivras-tu?

Quand je t'ai vue...: The picture was taken during the Expulsion.

CUSTOS, QUID DE NOCTE? CUSTOS, QUID DE NOCTE?

Drwy oriau'r nos, O lusern driw,
Ffyddlon y buost ti i'th Dduw:
Awr ar ôl awr, tra hunai'r byd,
Noswyliaist wrth dy Drysor drud.

Cedwaist dy Geidwad, Arial dlos;
Buost yn ddydd i'w dywyll nos:
Unig yw cwsg yr unig Un
Na ŵyr am gymar ar ei lun.

Cwmni'r digyfaill Gyfaill mawr
Yn ei dywyllaf dywyll awr,
Sefaist tra gorwedd yr oedd Dyn
Dan orchudd ebargofaidd hun.

Yn y distawrwydd unig, oer,
Dilyn a wnaethost siwrnai'r lloer:
Gwyddit pa bethau guddiai hon,
Pa lewyg pêr oedd dan ei bron...

Gwynfyd, dyhead, hiraeth dwys,
Gofid, ing, pryder, dagrau, chwys –
Gobaith ac ofn y ddynol-ryw
Fu'n llosgi'n fflam dy aberth byw.

Llosg, dirion lewych, lladd dy hun,
Dysg im fy ngwaith, O ffyddlon un:
Meudwy yr Iôr, hon yw fy swydd –
Ymlosgi, gwylied yn ei Ŵydd.

(Tôn: *Arizona*, 107)

VEILLEUSE

Burn on, burn on, thou faithful light,
All, all alone, watch through the night;
Stand by thy Master, stay awake,
Consume thy life-blood for His sake.

Thou art my teacher, silent flame:
Night, morn, noon, e'en, thou'rt e'er the same;
As earth rolls on in blissful sleep,
Faithful till death, thou'lt vigil keep.

Burn as Creation takes its rest,
Burn thou as burning eyes are blest
With Vision that none else may see,
Apocalyptic ecstasy.

Burn while the burning heart forlorn
Pants, palpitates, by sighing torn,
Crying aloud for someone's care,
Lying alone, for one not there.

Burn while the burning Fever kills,
Burn as the touch of Mœra chills;
Burn till Life's burning burns no more...
Burnt Youth! Press hard thine ageing whore.

O harbinger of rising Morn,
Glow as a glister's Spark is born:
Night after night, while æons last,
From soul to soul Life's torch is passed.

Lord, let me burn as this fair light,
Give, give my body day and night,
From hour to hour dissolve in love,
Shine till Aurora shine above.

(Melody: *Arizona*, 107)

FEMUR S. BENEDICTI... DENS S. BERNARDI

Yr esgyrn hyn y ddoe a rodiai'r llawr
Y safaf arno... Gwyddent a'r a wn
Yn nyfnder mêr fy nhebyg esgyrn 'nawr
Wrth ddechrau ar y rhyfedd fywyd hwn
A'u dug i'r fan lle maent... – Y fan lle maent!
O Dduw! A all mai gwir yw hyn, dy fod
Yn cadw acw 'nghudd i'th ethol Saint
– Ac i hwy'n unig – rod uwchlaw y rhod
Gyffredin i'r cyffredin ethol rai,
Bod graddau'n Uffern, graddau'n entrych Nef,
A graddau 'Mhurdan – fflam at bob rhyw fai
Na losgwyd eisoes, cyn mynd tua thref;
– Bod cwpan, fel y môr, yn llawn i'r pen,
Ond bod y môr yn dal holl ddafnau'r Nen?

Femur...: Cyfansoddwyd ar ôl gwaith glanhau'r creiriau.

263

(Opera Communia)

I spent an afternoon among the Saints.
They did not say a word, yet spoke to me
Of bygone days: of Martyrs' unheard plaints,
Of unseen Virgins' sealed virginity,
Confessors' proven virtue, Pontiffs' faith,
Of mine own Brethren now gone on before...
It was as though I bumped into the wraith
That still clung fast to every living pore
Of these used tools of Merit. I shook hands
With many who had worn what I now wear.
... And I thought hard o'er this small word that stands
Before the name of each life lying there:
Each his one life has had, his only one;
The one great Test has passed, the Title won.

TRWYN

Ddirgeled yw dy gudd gyfrinach di,
O beiriant bach, di-nod yr olwg, ond
Mor weithgar, heb yn wybod, bron, i ni
Ar hyd ein hoes, sydd, drwot ti, â'i llond
O'r harddwch hwnnw nad oes modd ei ddal
Â geiriau, na'i gyfleu â phaent neu liw:
Cans dy fân dyllau ydyw blychau'r wal
Sy'n amgylchynu cell yr enaid byw.
Fil gwaith, lleferaist wrthyf, heb 'r un sain,
Am Echdoe a adnabu dy glust gudd
O bell, o bell, trwy braffter trawst a maen
A gaeodd am y byddol Heddiw fydd.
Cans mae it gof mwy miniog na'r un un
O'th bewar brawd, i'r cof sydd wrtho'i hun.

1982

265

Wrth wrando ar yr Angelus

Cân, Angelus, cân dros y Clas,
Cân dyner gân yr oesoedd fu.
Arafa ennyd wallgof ras
Diddiwedd frys ein helbul ni.

Dy alwd glywir megis cynt
Bob bore, canol dydd a nos
Yn araf deithio tonau'r gwynt
Da gludo sain y Weddi dlos.

O blwyf i blwyf, o wlad i wlad,
Â allan gri'r angylaidd Wŷs:
"Am eiliad fer dy bryder gad,
Rho saib i'th enad, llacia'r brys.

"O! feibion dynion, beth yw lles
Yr holl waith wneir dros wyneb llawr
Heb gof o'r hyn sy'n dod yn nes
Nos ar ôl nos, wawr ar ôl gwawr?

"Myfi yw llais holl dynged Dyn.
Mae'r Dydd yn dod, a rhifo wnaf
Eich brysiog oriau'n un ac un –
Pa frys? – Mewn hedd i'r unlle'r af."

Myfi yw llais holl dynged Dyn...: Mae cloch oriau'r fam fynchlog yn
dwyn yr arysgrif:
LE JOUR DU JUGEMENT APPROCHE ET JE CONTE [sic] *LES HEURES.*

266

C'EST LE MOIS DE MARIE
(chantait Dom Isidore)

The Angelus rings out again
As it hath rung in bygone days,
As it now rings through France... through Spain...
Through every land that Christ obeys.

Three gentle notes of brazen song
Stop for a while this spinning Earth:
Each morn, noon, night, the years along
She halts, recalls her Maker's birth.

Awakened by the morning sound,
We hail the Maker of the Day:
Our knees and lips pressed to the ground,
We humbly kiss our native clay...

Whate'er the weight of each day's task,
The noon-day Call doth bid us pause
And Heav'n's calm, tender blessing ask
On Labour's unremitting laws...

And with the merciful dusk-light
We bid farewell to noise of words:
The sacred Silence of the night
Is sealed by three metallic chords.

From Angelus to Angelus
No sound may cross these fastened lips:
Alone, enshrouded, featureless,
Each head 'neath hooded blankness slips.

Cowl follows cowl without a word,
Each drifting slowly t'ward the Morn,
Until th'Angelic Cry be heard
Announcing distant rays of Dawn.

Hail Mary... – Hail! fair Morning Star,
Hail! Mother of the Break of Day:
With all my brethren, near and far,
My matin prayer to thee I say.

O Angelus! O Angelus!
Thou toyest with our earthly ball.
This worried world may fret and fuss –
Unchanged, thy cry shall Godward call.

(On melody composed for it)

BIENHEUREUX QUI PARLE
À DES OREILLES QUI ÉCOUTENT

Wrth wrando ar y llais am gwrendy i
A throi fy nghlyw i'r Clÿwr mawr ei hun;
Wrth ddofi clustiau f'enaid at y Si
Sy'n cludo dirgeleddau dyfnaf Dyn;
Wrth gofio pa fodd gynt y llanwyd hwn
Â lleisiau mân na wyddwn am eu bod
Gan amled, gyfarwydded oedd eu sŵn
A llawned gorlawn wacter aer fy rhod,
Mi welaf na bu imi weled dim
O'r Harddwch sydd i'w ffroenu 'nhonnau Sain,
Na gwybod effaith gudd trydanol rym
Y llef sy'n adlef i'r llef ddistaw fain.
Cans yn rhy aml gwrando wnawn â'm ceg,
A genau wnaed o'm clustiau'n araf deg.

1982

Mark 4, verse 9

How often have I brooded o'er the sound
That bears all others to the list'ning ear,
And brooding, new discoveries have found
'Mid th'emptiness that gently rumbles here...
This is the sound that bore in times gone past
The voices that were borrowed by my Lord
Who, as transmitting from some distant mast,
Used these as the conveyors of His word.
At times my two receivers were tuned in:
My *Input* was full on, and I received
Thy precious messages across the din.
At others not a whisper was perceived,
For though I turned the Volume, 'twas no use:
My *Output* system was far, far too loose.

Après avoir reçu les nouvelles de la Maison-mère

Dom Didier, que voyais-tu en l'air
Que tu traversais, tourné vers la mort?
On dit qu'à cet instant, en un éclair,
On entrevoit déjà son futur sort,
Qu'en un ou deux instants tout le passé
Repasse sur l'écran de notre vue,
Qu'avant l'atterrissage on sait assez
Déjà pour supputer ce qui est dû.
Ô Providence! Parfois l'heure est dure.
Les bambins de notre Ordre sont si peu,
Si peu nombreux! Sur vingt, un seul endure
Le traitement de cet étrange lieu...
... Ou as-tu prévu plus loin que nos yeux?
Le pire sait-il ce qui est de mieux?

Dom Didier: Jeune profès. Tout cela pour récupérer son bâton de spaciment!

HANDS

Will these one day be sealed with sacred oil
And bear within them pow'r to bless the world?
... La Trappe! Had I remained, a life of toil
Had worn these speakers of the silent word.
Yet here, as there, the hands replace the lung,
Though with a scribbled, not an acted, code.
Nay, even now they wield the dumb man's tongue,
And labour 'neath the lone heart's heavy load.
Sweet fettered hands! You held long, long ago
Things that you now reach out in vain to grasp,
And palped an hour what never more you'll know
Between the sensories of your unclaspèd clasp.
For that fair hold that could have held you fast
One eventide you waved into the past.

On ne doit jamais voir les mains

Pe na bai gen i'r rhain, ni fyddwn 'nawr
Lle'r wyf, cans nid eneinir a'r nad yw...
Pe collswn fel tydi, mewn ennyd awr,
A gollaist ddoe, ni fedrwn ddal fy Nuw.
Yn fach, bu ond y dim im golli un
O'r offerynnau hyn sy'n troi y byd –
Mân declyn, 'nawr fel gynt yn Cîteaux, sy'n
Dyrchafu'i lais di-adlais dros y mud.
Cyffyrddais fwy nag unwaith gyda'r rhain
Â'r hyn sy'n awr ymhell o'u gafael hwy.
Curiadau Rhythm a chyfaredd Sain
O guddiedigrwydd rhain ni ddeilliant mwy...
A'r trydan yng nghyplysiad bys â bys
Ni theithia mwy agendor marw flys.

1982

On ne doit...: Cyfarwyddwyd Meistr Newyddiaid la Trappe.
Pe na bai...: Mae'r Ddedf Ganonig yn gofyn am ddwlo di-nam.
Pe collswn, fel tydi,...: Cymrawd yn y nofisiaeth yn la Trappe.

NOS Y DYRCHAFAEL

(pedwar o'r gloch y bore)

Pan syllwyf ar y sêr uwchben
Sy'n gwylied mur y nefoedd wen,
Mi welaf law eu Crëwr hwy
Ac arni olion gwaedlyd Glwy'.

Cans heddiw, wedi'r deugain nydd,
Y traed a rodiodd hwn ein pridd,
A dyllwyd, rwygwyd ar y pren,
Sy'n dringo rhagfur sêr y nen.

Concwerodd! Â i menw drwy'r pyrth.
Gorchfygodd! Muriau'r nef a syrth
O flaen Cadfridog dynol-ryw,
Fu farw, 'nawr sydd eto'n fyw.

Y genadwri gwblhaed,
Gorchymyn Brenin nef a wnaed
Yn gyflawn – ie, sill wrth sill:
Arch-elyn Dyn ei deyrnas gyll.

Dychwelaist, Grist, o'r ffyrnig gad;
Dos, eistedd ar deheulaw'r Tad
Yn orfoleddus Aer y byd
Ryddheaist drwy dy friwiau drud.

Ymhell, ymhell uwchlaw y sêr
Mewn gwlad o bur oleuni pêr,
Na wyddwn ni ond am ei fod,
'Rwyt yno'n teithio'r bellaf rhod.

Ie, marchog, marchog arni fry:
Yn sain y Maranatha cry'.
O ben i ben y las Ysgrîn
Datguddier arwydd Mab y Dyn.

Fe'th farnwyd yma gennym ni:
Y diwrnod hwnnw, gennyt ti
Yr olaf lef ac adlef fydd
O nef i nef, i'r oesoedd cudd.

(Tôn: *Exsultet cælum laudibus*)

ASCENSION DAY
(after night office)

O empty sky! O silent night,
All filled with Peace and sacred Light,
How many stars dost thou contain?
Each seems to sing in quiet strain:
"We turn and turn for evermore
And nightly watch the sacred door
Of Heaven, 'gainst the powers of Dark,
And dance, the orbs of Time to mark.

"We are the joy of Him who cried,
'Let there be light!' – when Darkness sighed
To see his hold o'er th'æons lost
And then himself by rayons tossed
To Hell, where light no more doth shine,
Where Song gives place to Torment's whine,
Where th'incense is the very stench
Of rotting filth no flame can quench."

... And can it be that there, above,
The Author of all human love
Feels on this day some twinge of pain
And thinks of seeing once again
These hills that once those Feet did tread,
These hearts for which that Heart once bled,
These simple joys that life can give
To those who with its Giver live?

We are that faithful little band
The Father placed within thy hand:
Thou leavest us alone this day –
This is the parting of the way.
Rise up, above... above... above...
Thy Will be done... But come! sweet Dove,
Of which we heard that it was said
It would be given in his stead.

(On melody composed for it)

FAIM EST MEILLEURE SAUCE

Yr ympryd hwn a hogodd 'nawr dy fin,
Greadur mân a grewyd er creu Blas
Y Cread yn niflasrwydd alltud ddyn:
Am ddiwrnod crwn a hanner oedwyd ras
Y llwyth ar lwyth o frysiog brydiau llawn
A'th bylodd yn feunyddiol, hyd nes troi
Yn chwerw syrffed mêl melysaf ddawn
Y Rhoddwr na ddiolchir am ei roi.
Meddyliais dro na chaet fyth gyffwrdd mwy
Â rhai o'r rhoddion sydd o'm blaen yn awr:
Y 'menyn... y pysgodyn hwn... yr ŵy...
Rhwng muriau'r Trappe ni roddent byth eu sawr.
Ond aberth wnaf o'r aberth na chaf roi,
A mawl o'r Pleser baratowyd ddoe.

1982
(Gŵyl y Dyrchafael)

TASTE

It is a day of fasting, and the whip
Whacks through the air once more in every cell
Ere, yawning, once again we gently slip
Between our rugs to wait the morning bell...
It is a day of fasting, yet we'll eat
A little more than on a five course fast,
For on this day we'll feast upon the treat
Of knowing that the fast day is full past.
No milk, no cheese, no butter shall we see,
Nor shall at dawn or dusk aught come our way,
Yet what Delight in noon's frugality
For one who eats on a non-eating day!
Munch on, O World! Seek Epicure's own bliss!
Thou'lt never ever know what thou dost miss.

A day of fasting: Friday, but following Ascension Day. Vigils of solemnities have precedence over ordinary Fridays as regards fasting. In such cases, Friday has a simple dinner, with abstinence, but not supper or, of course, breakfast. (Dry bread and diluted wine, rather than water, is allowed in the evening on such Fridays.)

MEMORIES

When memories return once more
From whence they came, deep in the breast
That stores its bulging treasure store
Of yesterdays today that rest,
Then doth my spirit heave a sigh
And, sighing, touches whence 'twas heaved –
The depth of the unfathomed Cry
That none e'er heard or e'er perceived.

And in this sigh I feel once more
Hours that have walked into the Past
Walk back again, with bits of Yore
Beneath their steps still clinging fast
And marching past before mine eyes
In pageant after pageant bright
Of reincarnate living lies
That, mocking, dance before my sight.

... And when these spectred parts of Yore
Rouse in that unpreparèd breast,
That bursts 'neath its too bulging store,
Those yesterdays today that rest
Far, far more present than the Past
Was ever when it came this way,
Then yields that breast one mighty blast
Of Longing, for sweet Yesterday.

O Yesterday! how fair thou wast!
– Though little did I know it when
I let thee trickle slowly past
'Twixt these cupped hands which, now as then,
Receive, and lose what they receive,
Not knowing what they hold awhile,
No longer able to perceive
The Preciousness that Use makes vile.

Had I but known how to receive:
What 'tis to take, to open wide
The Emptiness that can't believe
The Gift that Someone doth confide
To its bared all – had I but known
That each new drop returned no more,
That in that Yesterday were sown
The Memories of evermore...

Then how, Oh! how would I have sucked
Each tiny dew-drop that distilled,
Would I have fondled each flow'r plucked
In that fair Paradise, that willed
To place before my new-found feet
Some unknown Hand that I knew not,
Saw not, nay, ne'er e'en paused to greet,
And soon 'mid all his gifts forgot.

O Yesterday! Come back again!
Lend me but one, one tiny hour,
Send upward thy descending rain,
Replant awhile each withered flow'r...
– Nay, 'tis absurd! This miracle
Omnipotence itself works not.
Time! – None e'er crossed this obstacle.
None; ever.
                    None!
                              Nay, one –
                                        Thou, Thought.

HOMO EST ANIMAL RISIBILIS

"Beth yw'r Gorchymyn Mawr?" un dydd medd Dad,
" 'Na chwardd', yntê?... A'r ail, cyffelyb yw:
'Na wena,' " – wrth im guchio (ar sarhad
Ei eiriau ar holl-sanctaidd eiriau 'Nuw)...
Ai gwir, fy Arglwydd, ydyw hyn, na fu
I'r sain anianol hon fyth groesi d'ên?
Ai gwiw'r athrawiaeth hon a ddaeth i ni,
Nad gweddus i sanct fynaich fwy na gwên?
– Ac eto, rhyfedd yw mai hwn yw'r nod
Sy'n gwahaniaethu Dyn o'i frodyr mud.
Rhydd perot air, ac eos gân i'th glod,
Ond nid effeithir un gan rymus hud
Y Goglais sy'n meddiannu oll a'i clyw...

Os Duw wnaeth hefyd hwn, Duw rhyfedd yw.

1982

"For homework... *think* of Laughter," said Miss Jones...
And so at home was what her namesake did.
He searched and searched until his very bones
Protested that the Mystery was hid:
What is it? What? What is't that sometimes works
While others fail to trigger off this chain
Of unexplained, unfathomable jerks
That, like small germs, can whole contingents gain?
No other creature knows this oddity
But Man – and even he, as th'authors say,
Should learn to walk above such crudity
And hold within the unmonastic neigh.
– Nay, Bernard! Hast thou solved what Miss did pose?
Is't shock, this thing that leaks through ear and nose?

Nay, Bernard...: Reference to St Bernard's description of the monk who, unable to contain laughter, lets it escape through ears and nostrils.

Ar ôl i'r newyddion dreiddio muriau'r Gell

Meddyliaf am dri gŵr y noson hon –
Ymhlith y mwya'n hanes prudd fy Ngwlad –
Y cyntaf, un a chwyddai don ar don
Ychydig cyn dydd geni 'Mam a 'Nhad:
Ysgytwr Cymru gyfan, ffŵl yr Iôr,
A ysodd Môn a Mynwy â'i wyllt dân;
Yr ail, ysgytwr byd o fôr i fôr,
A lwyddodd bron i'w chwalu'n deilchion mân;
Y trydydd? – Ti sy'n ysgwyd heddiw'n pridd
Â'th holl Slafonaidd egni: cans, fel 'rhain,
Fe ddaethost ti o hyd i'r ystryw gudd
Sydd mor effeithio heddiw ag o'r blaen.
Dowch, hybarch dri; dowch, dowch at dyrfa'r Sul
Yn hwyr... pan font o'r famwst oll yn chwil.

1982

THE WEDNESDAY OF THE DECISION

This is the day on which one little word
Doth choose the course of History, perhaps.
Today what Britain could so ill afford
Is to bear fruit, or utterly collapse.
John Paul, the whole wide world hath prayed for thee,
And waits this night to see which way shall turn
The cloud of incense that from sea to sea
The thurible of Prayer did fiercely burn.
And yet, is it a failure if it fails?
We have been so disgruntled at the grace
That Providence did offer heathen Wales
That men have spat in thine anointed face.
John Paul! – nay, Providence! – let it be *NAY*,
Till our stone hearts be grateful for a *YEA*.

Noswyl y Pentecost

Anialwch anial, diffaith, maith,
Dy ffin dd-ffin a'm deil yn gaeth.
A oes tu draw i'th orwel pell
Ryw wyrddlas dir, ryw wlad sydd well?

O! na bai cwmni ar y daith,
Cynhaliaeth ar y siwrnai faith,
Ond sain rhyw lais, neu gysur gwên,
Ymgeledd gwawr rhyw wyneb clên...

Ymlaen! Ymlaen! Rhaid mynd ymlaen,
Er gwaetha'r cur, yr haul, y straen,
Mewn llinel seth, heb ŵyro dim,
Gam ar ôl cam, hyd ddiwedd grym.

O! am ryw gysgod rhag y gwres!
Ai dŵr, ai rhith 'rwy'n gweld drwy'r tes?
A oes yn unman ffynnon glir?
A welaf eto ddynol dir?

Rhyw ardd ac iddi dyfiant ir!
Afonydd dyfroedd crisial pur!
O! sain adfywiol awel wynt...
O! gân fy mwyn ieuenctid gynt...

Ddi-gwmwl wybren, trugarha!
D'arteithiol oriau maith byrha!
Rho berl o wlith i enaid sych,
Â defnyn blaen fy nhafod gwlych –

Pa beth a wela'n codi draw?
Rhyw dawch? A all fod storm gerllaw,
Fod eto obaith arall ddydd
A dod o'r anial Angau'n rhydd?

Achubol Chwa, tyrd! Tyred! Chwyth!
O! Gwmwl gobaith, gad ond gwlith.
Pob dafn sydd berlen Bywyd pur –
Fwyn Awel! Hon dawela 'nghur.

(Tôn: *Veni, Creator Spiritus*)

WHITSUN

O living sacramental Life,
The same, whate'er the noise, the strife
Of Earth, of Time, of Human Kind –
An old, old Peace in thee I find.

The sight of those great outstretched hands...
The crimson form that yonder stands...
The sacred Stillness of my Lord...
The silence of the silent Word...

– The bell rings out: we bend the knee.
It rings again: we wait for Thee.
Thine epiclesis, Holy Ghost,
Draws Thee, yes Thee, into this Host

Thou broodest o'er the holy Gift
That holy hands now heav'nward lift,
'Tis Thou that unfelt, throbbing Force,
Of God's own birth the very source.

The great church bell with all its might
Announces thrice to inward sight
That He, the Lord of hosts, is here –
All now full-stretched, we lie, revere.

I am not worthy, Lord, to come,
To offer Thee my breast for home.
Should I stand back, and let Thee pass?
O Grace! O pentecostal Mass!

Nay, Spirit, come! I'll come. We'll meet.
Marana tha! My God I greet.
I kiss Thee, Lord, upon the lips,
Thy love outpoured my being sips.

The Holy Ghost has come to me:
Where there is one, there's Trinity.
The Spirit of my living Lord
Lives, breathes, moves, stirs – nay, more – is heard.

He calls me from the depth within:
"Behold the Bridegroom! Enter in.
This is the mystic nuptial bed.
Blest soul! thou'rt here with Blessing wed."

(*Veni, Creator Spiritus*)

The sight...: Carthusian rite. A reference also to first Mass seen through window of modern church at Oxford on this day in 1968.

Lines jotted on Whit Monday

"Remember me...," the lady said,
With tears beneath her failing eyes,
On that last night before I left,
That night of hid, repressèd sighs.

"Remember me," she said again,
Her wrinkled face now touching mine,
"When you're alone in that far cell..."
And harder pressed in tight entwine.

"Remember these our evenings spent
Together, in your student days,
When Youth and Age walked hand in hand
Before the parting of the ways."

"Remember..." – How could I forget?
Where art thou now, my aged friend?
At ninety-two where dost thou lie?
Thy wilting hours where dost thou spend?

Or doest thou listen as I write?
Art thou gone on where all must go?
Canst hear my young heart beating still,
The memories that haunt yet so?

"Ah! lovely boy!" I heard her groan,
As she squeezed harder, harder round.
O! voice of aged Virginity!
Unloved deep Love, I heard thy sound.

Age vanishes. It matters not.
The heart that hides in ev'ry breast
Beats, throbs, aches, pines throughout the years...
Unresting Eve, take now thy rest.

SOME STRAY LINES
(begun after the June examination)

The summer months have now begun,
Four full weeks' respite lies ahead:
The long semester's work is done,
The brain with Learning is well-fed.

How blissful is the moment when
Th'examiner says, *Finish now!*
The feeling of Release that then
The liberated mind doth know...

Vacation! Holiday! Repose!
– When I recall what these once meant
– Nay, what they mean e'en now to those
Who twelve whole months in toil have spent:

I ruminate o'er what this life
Contains for those who live it well –
The sound of Silence after Strife,
The alternance of heav'n and hell...

Variety! Ah! spice of Life!
Did people but perceive thy worth,
Did married man but see his wife,
Did happy souls know of their mirth...

– Alas! – 'Tis but the celibate
That knows the value of a ring;
And he for whom things alternate
No more, alone finds time to sing.

Could I but have my time again
And know but one more unknown dawn,
O! dazzled heart! how sweet the strain
With which thou'dst gather up the morn!

...And yet...! Couldst now this whole world see,
How great in fact would be the thrill?
– Is't not just this Man's misery,
No more to know how to sit still?

GŴYL SANT IAGO

O Ostyngeiddrwydd! Beth wyt ti?
Pa beth a fynni gennyf i?
Tyrd, tyrd yn agos ennyd mân,
Tyn orchudd du d'wynepryd glân.

Pam nad yngeni byth 'r un gair
Heb in dy holi di mor daer?
Pam na chlywn sill amdanat d'hun,
Na chŵyn na chri yn d'oriau blin?

Dwed, dwed beth yw'r gyfrinach ddofn.
Pam y fath swildod a'r fath ofn?
O! dirion forwyn, hawdd dy drin.
Ildio wnei'n syth dy farn dy hun.

Wele dy chwaer yn gwisgo'n ddel,
Â'i dwyfron noeth bob sylw'n hel.
Ai synnu wyt nad oes it ŵr,
Na 'nghlodydd byd y lleiaf stŵr?

Hardd ydwyt ti, a hardd dy chwaer,
Er – nid fel hi – na chredi 'ngair.
Ai, tybed, hwn yw'r harddaf oll,
I'r hon nas gŵyr, nad aeth yngholl?

(Tôn: *Duke Street*, 93)

FEAST OF ST JAMES

Didst thou once seek a place apart?
Hadst thou on glory set thy heart?
O son of thunder, thou'rt found out!
Man's silent heart the Truth will shout.

O unsophisticated youth!
Uncultured Galilean mouth!
Hadst thou not learnt the art of Pride,
That 'neath Humility must hide?

Come, little maid, disclose thyself;
Let down thy tresses, tiny elf.
Art thou afraid to be thus shown,
E'n to thyself thy grace to own?

See how thy sister flaunts her breast,
By all her lovers is caressed.
Art thou surprised thou'rt still unwed,
That none at thee e'er turned his head?

Why dost thou thus from people hide?
Why ne'er reply when men thee chide?
Why dost thou cede each victory,
E'en when 'tis thine the verity?

O quiet maid, how sweet thou art!
Locked, firmly locked, is thy sweet heart.
Ne'er on those lips heard I one *me*,
Nor speak they save they questioned be.

Was it of thee that Wisdom thought
When he two men of this once taught ?
Meekness! Is't thine the place of Pride
High, high on high, on Glory's side?

(Melody: *Duke Street*, 93)

Come, little maid...: The poem was inspired by memories of a walk
to Llangorwen church, where the virtues are depicted as virgins
in the little stained glass windows.

TRINITY SUNDAY

Why doth the heart of Youth so burn?
Why doth the old man's heart not learn?
Why doth this spinning world ne'er turn
    Within, within?

Love pumps Youth's palpitating heart –
Dreams that with Age grow dim, depart...
Sad child of Eve, how sad thou art
    Within, within.

Born of the earth, and earthly-born,
Made to be loved, unloved, forlorn,
This heart cries out, in pieces torn,
    Within, within.

No, no; no more is comfort found
In the great Void that doth redound
With echoes of the empty sound
    Within, within.

All, all without is passing..., passed;
Youth's deepest bliss one hour doth last...
O! heart of Man! No rest thou hast
    Within, within.

I turn aside and, weeping, cry
For some companion to draw nigh.
O! Essence! Heed th'unuttered Sigh
    Within, within.

Deep calls on deep, deep in this breast.
Made for its maker, 'twill not rest
Till it have seized Thee, Triune Guest,
    Within, within.

(Melody: *Almsgiving*, 420)

CORPUS CHRISTI

Is this the Bread that those fair Hands divided
  On that last night before they piercèd were?
Is this the Cup that Love itself provided
  For mortal thirst before it thirsted here?

Is this the Body? Is this the Blood?
Is this the Presence of the living God?

Hid is the essence of this hidden Manna,
  Hid from mine eyes – I see but bread and wine;
Yet on mine ears steal sounds of distant Cana
  Pow'r here at work, Authority divine.

Hearing alone can here be believed:
Sight, smell, touch, taste are utterly deceived.

Why stand I here e'er doubting, not believing,
  As he that asked the prints themselves to see?
Is Truth itself, like Man, deceived, deceiving?
  Will what it said not also come to be?

"This is my Body," said the Truth's own lips:
And 'tis His Blood that Man here gently sips.

Is not His word the law of all Creation?
  Has He not power o'er what His hands have made?
Age after age the Church in every nation
  On this strange Word her faith, her life, has laid.

For from the Twelve this faith she once received:
Will not their testimony be believed?

Nay, more, the Bridegroom keeps his Bride from error;
  Unto all truth, as promised, she is led.
Satan may bark; unshaken by his terror,
  Past Hell's own gates, untroubled she will tread.

This is her Faith. This is her very Life.
Man, do thy worst. She'll vanquish yet this strife.

Lord, I believe! I trust, I bend, I follow...
  Sight 'scapes my eyes, so strange a Bread I break:
That sinful Man the Son of God should hallow,
  And with a word the unmade Word should make!

Nay, 'tis too much! My heart will not withstand.
I hold who holds Creation in His hand.

                              (On melody composed for it)

MEDITATION ON THE LITTLE SHEET

Sleep on, my brother, take thy rest, 'tis o'er.
Far, far away repose from what awhile
Thou too didst know while yet on this same shore
Of Time, that laps each hour this desert isle
Called Solitude...

                 A hundred years have passed
And still it stands – alone in Chronos' sea.
I have, like thee, on her mine anchor cast
A day or two, unmapped of History.
Canst thou recall how once thou too didst stroll
O'er these baked sands that seemed so numberless,
How day on endless day did seem to crawl
From East to West, to endless Emptiness,
How far away did the Horizon seem
On which tonight this isle seems but a dream?

Little sheet: While dusting I came across a yellowing sheet
of paper in a rarely read volume. It bore a versified prayer to the
Sacred Heart on it. The author had left no signature, only the
date: *Feast of the Sacred Heart, 1882.* These are the words that
the little sheet bore:

> Within Thy Sacred Heart, dear Lord,
> My anxious thoughts shall rest;
> I neither ask for life nor death;
> Thou knowest what is best

Say only Thou hast pardoned me;
Say only I am Thine;
In all things else dispose of me;
Thy holy will is mine!

Ah! why is not my love for Thee
Unbounded, past control?
Alas! my heart obeyeth not
The impulse of my soul.

Ah! Jesus, if love's trusting prayer
Seem not too bold for Thee
Place Thine own Heart within my breast;
Love Thou Thyself in me.

Feast of the Sacred Heart,
1882

Day before visit

Five years have flowed beneath the bridge,
Five years, Youth's five last glowing years,
And once again those childhood tones
Will ring in this lone hermit's ears.

The time hath passed, unfelt, unknown,
And with it Youth's blest hours have gone,
Gone on their way to History...
I have not moved; yet I move on.

And so doth he whom soon I greet,
Whom I still see with vision clear
Before my solitary eyes
'Mid distant days to mem'ry dear.

We must go on, we have no choice.
We meet in Time and part again
To live another page of life...
We pause – ere Time its hold regain.

And so these little little feet,
Which I knew not, which had not walked
When I left uncreated life,
Will walk and talk where 'twas not talked.

For here the time hath passed not on.
The silence of these silent walls
Doth testify that nought doth change
In each Today that softly falls.

We meet again... We part again...
This Joy that we *Encounter* call
Embraces Past and Present tears
One hour... ere Future onward haul.

FEAST OF ST MARY MAGDALENE

And can it be that this Carthusian heart
    Was made for love?
Did it rest cold as our two ways did part
    To meet above?
And were those hands that waved and waved again
    Till out of sight
Stretched out that night in vain?

Nay, even as I write two big, big tears
    Roll down my cheeks.
The grinding Roller of inhuman years
    No respite seeks.
You have grown old, and will grow older still:
    The end begins,
And doth my life-source kill.

... And thou, my friend!... Where lies that unkissed head
    On this warm night?
The flame that welded us, is't wholly dead,
    Forgotten quite?
Did we not sense what unsparked Life could mean
    When we said *No* –
 Yet glimpsed what might have been?

Thou too hadst heard the charmed faint siren Cry,
    And hadst been torn.
That flowing hair that should 'neath wimples lie
    Still danced unshorn.
Thy body craved an earthly bridegroom – nay,
    E'en though thy soul
      Knew where full rapture lay.

Fade, fade, thou unknown, unused virgin breast
    From memory's sight.
Forget an hour when heart 'gainst heart was pressed
    And Truth held tight,
When two closed eyes bid that Truth nothing say,
    But just be only be,
      For 'twas Farewell, for aye...

... And as I saw the last of those green hills
    Sink 'neath the crest,
Did not I feel the wrestling of two wills
    Within my breast?
Is't nought but soil that makes us what we are?
    O! Wales! O! Wales! –
      So near, yet so far.

Alone, alone, I hear the distant chime
    Call me to sleep.
Another day begins, another time,
    Yet I still weep.
Nay, nay, the hermit's heart beats loudly too:
    I love Thee, Lord –
 Thy world my love doth woo.

                     (Melody: *Lux benigna*)

The end begins...: Written after seeing my brother's car disappearing in the distance and hearing of our father' s illness.

AR ÔL GWELD CAR FY MRAWD YN DIFLANNU YN Y PELLTER
(a chlywed am salwch Dad)

Wrth gofio'r nos y croesais ffin fy ngwlad
    Am estron dir,
Cudd ddagrau 'Mam ac olaf wên fy Nhad
    A wela'n glir.
Y dwylo mwyn a'm magodd aent yn llai...
    Yn llai, llai fyth...
    Ond chwifient heb wanhau.

Y diwrnod hwnnw clywais acen ffrind
    O'r Gogledd pell,
Llais geneth dlos, yr olaf cyn im fynd
    At ddiwair gell.
Y dewis waned; dwy aelwyd ddeuai'n dlawd:
    Yr un a'm gwnaeth
    A'r un na wnaeth fy nghnawd.

Darllenais weddi'r bore hwnnw – do,
    Yng nghlustiau 'mhlwy',
O flaen yr Allor yn addoldy'r fro
    Na welwn mwy –
Yr Allor honno fu cyhyd yn dyst
    Im holl ddyheu
    Am bêr gynteddau 'Nghrist.

Yr anwes olaf hwnnw deimlaf 'nawr
        Yn dal yn dyn.
Tra pery 'nghof i'm llygaid eto daw'r
        Atgofion hyn
Am ddwylo mynach, breichiau lleian bur
        A'm carai'n ddwfn,
        A'm dug at draed y Gwir.

Af yn eu camre hwy yn llwybrau'r Saint
        At Wlad sydd well.
Ffarwél, fy Nghymru! D'erwau, cilio meant
        Dros orwel pell.
Ffarwél! Ffarwél! 'Rwy'n gadael annwyl bridd
        Fy mebyd cu
        Am gyfandiroedd Ffydd.

Ond a oes rhan ohonom eto'n bod
        Lle buom gynt?
Y pethau bychain hyn sydd weithiau'n dod
        Ar donnau'r gwynt –
A fynnant dynnu ar yr hyn a'n gwnaeth
        Yr hyn yr ŷm
        A'n gwneud i ddeule'n gaeth?

(Tôn: *Lux benigna – Lead, kindly light*)

The twenty-ninth of July, 1981

On this day (that of the marriage of the Prince of Wales) was written the poem which figures on the eighth of December (*Immaculate Conception*), with the difference that the seventh stanza once ran thus:

How doth it feel, O uncreated king,
To wake and find what unearned Luck doth bring?
– Yet, is not this the gift of each new morn
To unawakened dreams, undreamt, unborn?

The sixth of August

To this high place, my loving Lord,
Thou led'st me by Thy loving word.
Finger of God, that plucked my heart,
Thou brought'st me here, apart... apart...

... Apart from all that is not Thee,
Apart from what one day must flee;
Apart from men, apart from life,
Apart from Love, Youth, Friendship, Wife...

Tabor! Alone I stand on thee:
God, God alone looks down on me.
Naked I lie, I wait, I cry;
Bare with bare truth, for Truth I sigh.

Stripped of my self, I have no more;
Stranded, I stand on this world's shore.
Upward alone may I now look –
Nay! Heav'n itself heav'n from me took.

Nought, – nought! nought! nought have I left now.
Wisdom! walk on: to Thee I bow.
Walk o'er me, Lord; pass by, pass by...
My will is Thine. I ask not *Why?*

Mountain of God, Man hears on thee
The silence of the Silent Three.
O God! Great God! Thou speakest not.
The wind blows on... Man lies forgot.

...Or can it be – ? Is't here that starts
The meeting of two broken hearts:
Thine own – because I knew not Thee,
And mine – on Tabor's Calvary?

(Melody: *Hesperus*)

The Silent Three: The Transfiguration is one of the rare occasions when the whole Trinity is made manifest.

Y PYMTHEGFED O AWST

Ai gwir y troediais innau gynt
Lle troediodd Duw, lle clywyd gwynt
Rhyw chwa o'r glas ehangder maith
Y nos daeth diwair fron yn llaith?
A sefais yn yr union fan
Y safodd cennad arall lan
Arhosai am ond sill, ond gair
O dawel enau'n hannwyl chwaer?

A glywais i'r di-amser Si
Gyffyrddodd gynt â'i chlustiau hi
Pan ganai gyda lleisiau'r gwynt
Wrth ddwyn o'i mewn eu crëwr hwynt?
O eneth dlos, a genaist di
Dragwyddol Gân Ieuenctid cu?
A deimlaist dithau dan dy fron
Wefr merch i'r Greadigaeth hon?

A'm gwyry fwyn, ai gwir yw hyn,
Y dringaist dithau unwaith fryn
Addurnwyd gan fudreddi dyn
At gamre pur y puraf un?
Ai yma yn y fangre hon
Yr aeth y cleddyf drwy dy fron?
O Fair! O Fair! A weli'n awr
Y fan y plygaist dithau i lawr?

A hefyd, Mair, ai gwir yw hyn,
Y bu it ddringo arall fryn,
A chodi dy heirdd lygaid du
At gwmwl a esgynnai fry –
A bod i dithau yn dy dro
Ymadael â'th anwylaf fro,
Nid yn dy ddagrau megis cynt,
Ond gyda chwa rhyw nefol wynt?

(Ar dôn y Tad Lawrence)

The fifteenth of August

Did once those little, little feet
Walk, run, play, dance from street to street
In that enbalmèd promised land
Where Earth and Heav'n walked hand in hand?
And did that tiny infant breast
That ages would one day call blest
Beat, palpitate at Childhood's joys
And fondly hug its simple toys?

Did that dark hair blow in the breeze
Beside those Galilean seas?
And did that tender full-bloomed rose
Know what each growing maiden knows?
And was th'eternal Song of Youth
Heard in that gentle, gentle mouth?
And couldst thou know what waited thee,
Locked womb of locked Virginity?

And did she know a harder time?
Did that rose droop 'neath fiercer clime?
And did the depth of that deep heart
One day cry out, torn, ripped apart?
And didst thou, Mary, hear thy son
Say *Woman!* and cry out *'Tis done! ?...*
Sweet breast, wast healed, or rent anew
As who had milked thee smaller grew?

And Mother, where dost thou lie now?
What secrets doth that breast now know?
And is it true, as these men say,
That thou didst leave us on this day,
Not as a common child of Eve
That, gasping, doth one last breath heave,
But as a queen, with seraph train –
That little feet o'er æons reign?

(Melody: Fr Laurence's tune for *Christmas Night*)

GWYNETH

Pluck thy wild roses ere they fade,
While thou'rt yet young fill thy full breast
With th'incense that thy Lord hath made
To rise for thee from Eden Blest.

Thou'lt never come this way again:
This Happiness thou now dost know
Is of a distant Yesterday
That with Tomorrow's tide shall flow.

This is the day of days for thee,
The daylight of all days to come,
The twilight of the days that flee
'Mid mem'ries of thy frst morn's home.

Nay, look into the Past one hour
Ere't be for e'er beyond thy grasp:
These hands that tended thee, sweet flow'r,
Now lose thee in another's clasp.

The day will come when thou in turn
Shalt part with what was made of thee.
This flame that doth in thee now burn
Thou'lt hand on to eternity.

Thou'rt but a runner in the Race:
The torch of Life is given thee
One hour... Run hard. Keep up the pace...
Then pass it on to History.

For though thou know it not, thou too
Dost turn this day a well-marked page.
This chapter many, many knew:
Thou'rt at the zenith of all age.

Accept, accept, with all thy pow'rs,
The Gift that passes now through thee.
Of all Time's endless, timeless hours,
This one is thine.

                          It had to be.

WRTH YMBARATOI AT Y CYMUN
(fore Sul)

O Risiart Gwyn, pa beth ddigwyddodd it
Pan ddaethost 'nôl o Fwrdd y Cymun gynt?
Ai Protestant, ai Catholigwr wyt?
Paham yr aethost dro ar estron hynt?
Pa beth sydd orau, Cymun nad yw'n bod
Ai Cymun na chei gael, er d'holl ddyheu?
Ti deimlaist effaith y Cysegriad od
A'r Gwir Absennol fedrai ond gyfleu.
Cysegriad od! Rhagluniaeth odiach fyth!
Er paratoi cnawd un at ddur a mwg
Ti elwaist bâr o gigfrain gwyllt o'u nyth
Er mwyn cyfleu dy wir bresennol Wg –
I bigo allan ddarn wrth felltith ddarn
O'r anghysegriad ddatgysegrodd Barn.

1982

DURING THANKSGIVING
(Sunday morning)

I have a friend who, as I hold this pen,
Holds in his hands the Bread that they have blessed.
Saint Richard, he and thou are Oxbridgemen,
And he, like thee, Christ's Presence hath confessed
Before these altars where thou'dst Him receive,
That stand unchanged to witness to the Change
That changing times have changed – as did believe
The ravens that did work this work so strange.
O Teacher, answer one last child's remark.
This word that this good priest once quoted me –
"A Presence we too hold, yet it demark
And it define we'd not, as it likes thee," –
Can it hold true? Nay, hath it any sense?
Doth what one *holds* change unchanged Absence dense?

The ravens: The reference is to the story of St Richard Gwyn. Two ravens pecked cruelly at his stomach after he had received the Anglican Communion, and he vowed he would never do so again. He was eventually martyred, but the local people were unwilling to prepare the gallows of their well loved teacher.

Après avoir reçu une lettre de Jean-Philippe

Ah! quand je vois de nouveau ces grands murs
Qui abritèrent un ou deux beaux jours
Ma bleue jeunesse et qui – j'en étais sûr –
Allaient encor l'abriter pour toujours,
Les souvenirs... les souvenirs... reviennent
En foule... en autre foule, encor plus dense
Que tout ce que ces autres murs contiennent
De Vacuum gonflé de pure absence.
Ah! Ah! cet idéal qui m'alluma
Un jour d'été n'est toujours pas éteint.
O! nue d'inconaissance que, là-bas,
Mon cœur inconnu eût connue, sans fin!...
– Perpétuel Silence! Ah! pas un bruit
Jusqu'à la mort, pour trahir qui je suis.

Yr Wythfed o Fedi

O dirion Fun, ar gyfryw orig fwyn
Gwelaist a chlywaist gyntaf lun a swyn.
Beth ddaeth i'th feddwl, beth oedd d'argraff di
Wrth ddod at lewych dydd o'r dywyll fru?

O Enedigaeth! Gwyn dy felys fyd!
Newydd yw ffrwd dy ffynnon bêr o hyd.
Newydd yw'r Rhodd a newydd ydyw'r Gwlith
Sy'n tawel ddisgyn oddi fry'n ddi-lyth.

Nos ar ôl nos cofleidia nef a llawr:
Aer bythol Nef wneir mewn nefolaidd awr,
Derbyn, ond derbyn, yw swyddogaeth Dyn –
Gronyn o'r Duwdod wna dduw ar Ei lun.

Munud, na, eiliad, digon yw i'r wyrth:
Holl rymusterau'r Gofod iddo syrth.
Ddoethineb! Dirgel dy gyfrinach gudd –
Sibrwd a wnei... Sibrydiad, einioes fydd.

Minnau a ddeuthum hefyd yn fy awr:
Oesoedd di-oes a'm dug at oriau'r Wawr.
Efa ei hun a'm cludai dan ei bron –
Mab wyf i feibion yr hen famwys hon.

O Efa newydd, Afe yw fy nghân!
Henffych it heddiw, faban annwyl, mân!
'R un yw dy darddiad di â'm tarddiad i –
Henaist o'r Hanfod sydd yn hanu fry.

Tyf, tyf at lawnder, tyf at lewyrch oed,
Gwêl beraidd ardd Ieuenctid wrth dy droed;
Ddydd ar ôl dydd cofleidia ddawn yr Iôr,
Nofia, ymollwng yn y neithdar Fôr.

Os bychan wyt, nid bychan wyt i ni:
Eglwys yr oesoedd cuddio mae'n dy fru.
Dy ddwyfron fach sydd wynfydedig, Fair:
Ti yw ein pen, ein mam, ein ffrind, ein chwaer.

(Tôn: *Eventide*, 211)

THE EIGHTH OF SEPTEMBER
(1981: a distraction during morning study)

Now as I write I think again
How at this hour on this great day
I took one step o'er one small stone
And left the world behind for aye.

Elev'n o'clock was striking then
As it rings now within mine ears –
The only sound that I have heard
Through these five solitary years.

Ring on! – I listen to your song.
Ring on! – Your voice alone may speak.
Ring on! Ring on, as you have done
Each quart... each hour... each day... each week...

O Sound of Time! – the only sound
That reaches a Carthusian's ears –
Thou knowest not, as every hour
Thou strikest, what its joys, its tears.

To thee each one is as the last:
It comes... it goes... it comes again,
As round and round thou turnest me
While Sun doth rise and Moon doth wane...

O Lord, my Lord, did Jewry too
Have engines that their makers rule
Long, long ago when Thou wast here
In Solitude's unchangèd school?

Y PEDWERYDD AR DDEG O FEDI
(Gŵyl y Grog)

O henffych well! anwylaf Groes,
Ti unig obaith ein hoes!

Llewyrcha dros y moroedd,
Teyrnasa dros ddynol-ryw;
Cofleidia, casgla'r bobloedd
Dan gysgod adain ein Duw.

   Hosanna! Henffych, fwyn Bren!
   O grog, tydi fyddi ben.

Mwyn gysgod mewn diffeithwch,
Mynecbost i enaid coll;
Mewn cynnwrf mange heddwch,
Cysgriad ein croesau oll.

   Rhyddhad! Do, daeth in ryddhad.
   O felltith! Ti gei'r mawrhad.

Ti ddeliaist ar dy freichiau
Y Breichiau a ddaliai'r byd;
Dy droed odd allor Meichiau
Iawn-daliad ein dyled ddrud.

Concweraist! – a choncoro wnei.
O Artaith! Ti Wynfyd gei.

Anwesaf heno'r olion
Lle lladdwyd Angau ei hun.
Cusanaf fan yr hoelion
Gaethiwodd Ryddhawr Dyn.

O Grocbren! Ti ferni'r byd.
O Gariad! Gorchfygaist Lid.

O Arwydd Iachawdwriaeth,
Fe'th welir ryw ddiwrnod fry.
Tan hynny'n dy filwriaeth
Ymladdwn dan d'astalch di.

Gorffennwyd! Rhwygwyd y Llen!
Mae'r ffordd yn rhydd at y Nen.

(Tôn: *Victoire! Tu règneras.
Ô Croix, tu nous sauveras!*)

The fourteenth of September

Hail, Glory! Hail, glorious Tree!
O Cross, thou hast set us free!

Shine o'er the vast Creation,
Illumine Earth's starless night,
Assemble every nation
Beneath thy radiant light.

> Hail, Glory! Hail, glorious Tree!
> O Cross, thou hast set us free!

O! arms of consolation,
Reach out across all the years!
Mankind's sole consolation
Down Time's dark chasm of tears.

> Hail, Glory! Hail, glorious Tree!
> O Cross, thou hast set us free!

O! sweet, sweet little acorn
Predestined for such a tree!
The death-bed of Life's first-born,
The seed of Eternity.

> Hail, Glory! Hail, glorious Tree!
> O Cross, thou hast set us free!

Blest Wood, thy blessèd furrows
Against my lips let me press.
These prints felt my Lord's sorrows,
To these was nailed Love's caress.

> Hail, Glory! Hail, glorious Tree!
> O Cross, thou hast set us free!

Stand o'er our constellation,
Await, await there on high;
And then, Sign of Salvation,
Appear in our crumbling sky.

> Hail, Glory! Hail, glorious Tree!
> O Cross, thou hast set us free!

Here, for an understanding of the metrics, is the original French version:

Victoire! Tu règneras!
Ô Croix! Tu nous sauveras.

> *Rayonne sur le monde*
> *Qui cherche la Vérité,*
> *Ô Croix, source féconde*
> *D'amour et de liberté.*

Victoire!...

> *Redonne la vaillance*
> *Au pauvre et au malheureux;*
> *C'est toi, notre espérance,*
> *Qui nous mèneras vers Dieu.*

Victoire!...

> *Rassemble tous nos frères*
> *À rombre de tes grands bras,*
> *Par toi, Dieu notre Père*
> *Au ciel nous accueillera.*

Victoire!...

Holy Rood Day (very ancient, connected with the discovering and venerating of the True Cross after the cessation of persecutions) is the beginning of the monastic Lent. The above is a well-known French hymn.

GŴYL SAN MIHANGEL A'R HOLL ANGYLION

Wrth imi wrando ar sibrydiad Heddwch,
Dyfnder y nos a dafnau'i dwys lonyddwch,
Teimlaf unigedd trwchus y tywyllwch
     O gylch fy enaid.

Distaw yw'r gell, a distaw ydyw'r Gofod,
Distaw yw cwmni'r anweledig Hanfod,
Di-air yw ymgom dirgel ymgyfarfod
     Enaid ac enaid.

Ie, ai unig ydyw cri fy nghalon?
Ai hi yn unig ŵyr am ei gofalon?
Neu a oes un ynghudd yn su'r awelon
     A glyw fy enaid?

A all mai hwn yw siffrwd mân adenydd
Rhyw gyfrin ffrind yn gwarchod fy ngobennydd
Ac, er y gwyll, yn darllen llyfr f'ymennydd
     A'n gweld fy enaid?

Na, na, nid unig heno mo'r anialwch:
Rhwng muriau'r gell mi glywaf drwy'r tawelwch
Fyrdd myrddiwn olau'n gwibio drwy'r tywyllwch –
     Bob un yn enaid.

(Tôn: *Christe, Sanctorum decus Angelorum*)

MICHAELMAS

Am I alone in this unreal Silence
'Twixt these great walls, unstormed by this world's violence?
When with one click I drive out noisy radiance,
    Am I in darkness?

Is there a Light, unknown of human feeling,
Over my resting head some Presence kneeling,
Stooping at whiles, at others glances stealing
    At unknown Beauty?

This tingling Void that patters on the ear-drum,
Th'echoing Yawn of Solitude's huge Boredom,
Is it but Sound, or are there found 'neath th'hours' hum
    Glisters of Meaning?

What is it? Light? Force? Breath? Ethereal Spirit?
Or but a friend that christened souls inherit?
What of the world? Can others also merit
    Angels of Glory?

Matins are sung, and Dawn o'ertakes my vigil.
Waking I sleep, and think upon thee, Angel,
Knowing thee there, yet finding not the angle
    At which to pierce thee.

1981

(Melody: *Christe Sanctorum decus Angelorum*)

Y PUMED O HYDREF
(chwarter wedi saith yr hwyr)

Mae'r Eglwys heno'n hardd ei gwedd,
Yn deg ei gwisg ar gyfer gwledd
Ein Hurdd, ein tŷ, ei teulu ni –
Sant annwyl! daeth dy noswyl di.

Am deirawr canwn donau d'Urdd –
Y siant a ganodd myrdd ar fyrdd
O'th blant diepil, oes 'rôl oes,
Dan nod y ddigyfnewid Groes.

Mewn abid seml, gwyn o wlân,
Yn sain y gyfareddol gân,
Fe'n hunir â'r cycyllog lu
O fudion leisiau'n canu fry...

Yr un sillafau, nodau, swyn,
Yr un aroglau gweddi'n dwyn
Hyd nef y fythol litani,
Hen, hen fawreddog litwrgi.

O salm i salm, o awr i awr,
Fe'n tawel gludir at y Wawr,
Gan ddilyn yr ormdaith faith
A'n herys fry ar decach traeth.

Dof ar dy ôl, O Batriarch:
Heb enw ar fy nghroes, heb arch,
Fe gysgaf wrth eu hochr hwy,
Yn angof ddoe... yn angof mwy...

(Tôn: *Serve Dei/Martyr Dei)*

The sixth of October

O BONITAS! – Was this thy cry?
Was this thy goodly spirit's sigh
On seeing one reflection of
That measureless unmeasured Love?

Nay, measureless was thy love too;
Love's gamble that gay spirit knew:
The *ALL* – and nothing but the *all* –
A smaller bet were risk too small.

The Absolute was all it knew:
Half-hearted love were love untrue...
Magnetic monk of Chartreuse Mount,
Thy progeny in myriads count!

O festive face! We follow thee
'Neath *stable Cross* to victory;
With banded cowl and pointed hood
We stand where generations stood...

And sing the song of Sacrifice
Through summer sweat and winter ice,
Month after month, year after year
Repeating Repetition here.

O Patriarch! Thou livest still:
This city built upon a hill
Hath stood, doth stand, shall stand again
Till Hiddenness high glory gain.

(Melody: *Martyr Dei qui unicum*)

After hearing of B...'s pilgrimage

Is't possible that but four weeks ago
A figure once well-known, nay, known too well,
A bosom that once knew all that I know
(Whose warmth warmed once too often this cold cell)
Could once again be seen of waking eyes
Beyond the trellis of fenced chastity,
That these dumb espions of unwitnessed sighs
Did separate one hour Eternity
From Time, from passing Time, from bliss in Time,
From earth, from earth's own Life, from life on earth,
And from two feet that once again did climb
In search of that embrace of unlaced mirth,
That has not been forgotten, nor can be,
For though these walls be thick, they did feel thee.

16/7/82

Le même, la nuit

Ma sœur, quand je t'ai vue ce soir en rêve,
J'ai cru revivre une heure de la nuit
Où, angélique, et pourtant seconde Ève,
Tu vins m'offrir un goût de ce doux fruit
Que toi aussi tu reçus de ta Mère.
Nuit après nuit on parlait, face à face,
Et parfois tu m'embrassais comme un frère,
Mais ce soir-là ta Chair dit: *Qu'on m'embrasse!*
... Un autre saura-t-il ce que j'ai su
Alors, quand au-dedans j'ai dit: *Non! Non!* ?
Un autre verra-t-il ce que j'ai vu –
Que, même toi tu as ce que tous ont?
– C'est pourquoi j'ai détourné mon regard
De cet Éden
          – Qui revint,
                     – Mais trop tard.

After Reverend Father's refusal

And I had thought that it would be for e'er
When once, still green with Youth's first beaming smile,
I looked not back at what again ne'er, ne'er
I'd see – those angel forms I'd loved awhile –
But at the Cross, that standing on the world,
And took it for my bride, my only Friend,
The one that would stand firm as all else whirled,
For I had vowed to bear it to the end.
But now that world is crumbling round my ears,
And what I thought changed not now slowly blears.
In one short morn the length of sev'n long years
Has flowed away 'neath torrents of hot tears.
O thick Unknown! I walk alone, alone
From what I knew so well that 'twas not known.

21/3/84

THE TWENTY-FIFTH OF MARCH

This is the day that changes all my days,
And makes me what so long had seemed untrue.
La Trappe! Who, who could e'er have known the ways
That were to bring me back to thee, and you
My quiet, quiet brethren, who still smile
As you did smile before, from 'neath your hood,
At one that knew your goodness for a while
And cast it off, to seek an alien good.
I have come home, and in your arms I feel
Th'embrace that said, *Goodbye; but thou'lt return.*
O massive walls! O Altar! Here I kneel,
As long, long, long ago, where't 'gan to burn.
And thee, my father! In thy arms I cried,
For thou wast right. And yet I tried.

I tried!